SHIFT IN PROGRESS

SHIFT IN PROGRESS

Faith Principles for
Your Journey Through Destiny

Harry Rhau

Shift in Progress

Copyright © 2021 Harry Rhau

Produced and printed by Stillwater River Publications.

All rights reserved. Written and produced in the United States of America. This book may not be reproduced or sold in any form without the expressed, written permission of the author and publisher.

Visit our website at www.StillwaterPress.com for more information.

First Stillwater River Publications Edition
ISBN: 978-1-952521-94-2
1 2 3 4 5 6 7 8 9 10

Written by Harry Rhau.
Published by Stillwater River Publications,
Pawtucket, RI, USA.

The views and opinions expressed in this book are solely those of the author and do not necessarily reflect the views and opinions of the publisher.

To my Pastor Wesley Wagnac thank you for the spark that lit the fuse to the idea for this book and many more to come.

To my siblings I love you. Vallerie your love for me is undeniable, especially that night I cascaded off the front end of that car. Everyone heard you scream. My brother William, I wanted to be like you when we were kids and the little brother in me still does. Michelle, my first best friend you are a flower that is still blooming.

My father, my Pastor, Jean Gerard Rhau thank you for your example. You read to us when we were kids. The gift of a book on my 21st birthday reinvigorated my love for reading and brought me to this moment of writing my own.

To my mother Esther Rhau, you worked 3rd shift many years for us. I thank you. You prepared dinner early so you could sleep during the day to get rest for your nights at work. Every now and again you would call me from outside where I was playing. You would have me kneel down at your bedside to pray for me. Whatever you have prayed for has come to fruition.

To my beautiful wife Charlene, I love you dearly. You've been my number one support from day one. Thank you for your companionship and your devotion to personal authenticity. It has taught me much. Thank you for my two children Nahlia Cadence Rhau and Janeas Harrison Rhau. They are a testimony of God's grace in our lives.

To my eternal Father God, I want to be just like you because my children want to be like me.

CONTENTS

Chapter 1	Paradigm Shift	1
Chapter 2	Training Wheels	12
Chapter 3	Hunger	29
Chapter 4	Long Faith	46
Chapter 5	Fighting Faith	55
Chapter 6	Know Thyself	67
Chapter 7	Target Focus	90
Chapter 8	Future Oriented to Present Minded	108
Chapter 9	Don't Miss The Shift	125

Chapter 1
Paradigm Shift

As this book came into development, the onset of a global pandemic showed its ugly head. COVID-19, also known as coronavirus, was ravaging lives here in the US but also abroad. I never imagined that my generation would see this sort of impactful set of events. All of society was forced into quarantine and I would be remiss if I did not address this life-changing epidemic.

If there is one thing I believe to be true in the midst of all this uncertainty, is that things will never be the same when this pandemic ends. Currently all schools are closed and have transitioned to online classes. All businesses have been shut down except "essential" establishments like grocery stores, gas stations, and pharmacies. The economy is at a standstill, but a stimulus package of up to six trillion dollars was approved to bailout big corporations, small businesses, and offer small checks for families affected.

In this time a new vocabulary term has been adopted into the mainstream: social distancing. Because of this virus people are required to remain in quarantine, but if they need to come out they must maintain a distance of six feet from the nearest person. Going into public, you find most, if not all, wearing a mask and gloves. I may have washed my hands more during the pandemic than I have my entire life. All sorts of normal face-to-face communication has been reduced to Facetime and Zoom conferences. Hospitals are very restrictive and are only allowing one visitor for patients. It has been most unfortunate for the loved ones of people who have passed away during this time, whether it be from coronavirus, natural causes, or other circumstances. Those who have died are unable to receive proper home going services in their honor. Churches are closed and large gatherings of people are outright prohibited. Handshakes, hugs, and kisses are a death sentence in this time, and do not even think about coughing or sneezing in public.

I could go on, but it's been established that Coronavirus has brought about complete and total change. In so many ways it has brought the world to its knees. One thing noone can deny is things will not be the same when it is all over. A shift is on the horizon. While this may be a negative, unpleasant circumstance, I know that many good things can come from this. I can also say the same about your life as well. The most significant things in your life and maybe even small innocuous details are not the result of mere happenstance.

God uses the greatest and the smallest things that occur in your life as a reminder to you that there is a shift in progress.

When you get in the car to go somewhere you know every turn you are going to make in order to reach the destination. Even when you are going somewhere you have never been there is a GPS you can follow and it gives you the step-by-step until reaching that place. In that same way you should have a goal. You need to have a target. If you do not, then you will wander aimlessly. When you are pressing towards a mark your steps need to be calculated.

Someone close to me was sharing with me how he was able to purchase a new home. He was having a hard time in his finances and life circumstances. He was taking care of his wife and children but he was struggling. He wanted a bigger home for his four children to play and where they were was too small for them. I asked him what he thought was the disconnect between praying, keeping a positive mindset, and actually seeing results. This was his response:

It's hard to speak on people's personal experiences but for me I can say that in the very recent past,

I thought I was thinking positive but not really.

For example, before last year, I kept saying, "I do not make enough money.....when I make enough I can get a house in five years."

That may sound positive in a way, but I was selling myself short. Staying with that mentality would guarantee that it would take five years or more to achieve that goal.

Last year a series of events led me to change my mentality. I told myself that next year by the end of the summer I will be in a new home that I purchased. It was an overwhelming thought. I did not have a clue how... But I knew that it was possible and that I wanted it badly for my family. People who are discouraged and intimidated by dreams and goals sell themselves short, and literally are the very reason why they do not accomplish anything.

For me it was a step-by-step process. I knew I needed a certain credit score to even get pre-approved, so my focus was on that in the forefront. House still in my mind, I shortly realized that to boost my credit I had to learn what it was and how to raise it. So I learned everything about credit score, etc. Once I felt confident in my knowledge of credit I then focused on taking action on what I had learned. In order to take action, I needed money. I applied to Amazon warehouse in Massachusetts and was going to work an extra twenty-plus hours, and it was an hour's drive each way.

Crazy thing is, I requested time off to go to an Amazon orientation because I got hired. As I normally do, I request the time and put the reason for the time off. I wrote "Amazon orientation."

That set off a whole chain of events that led my manager to approach me. She let me know that I am not supposed to know, but Eric, owner of the company, was going to call me into his office and offer me more money. I was surprised and confused and did not really understand why. So later I was asked to meet with Eric, acting surprised of course.

He said, "What's up? How are you? We just gave you a raise, are we not paying enough?"

I assured him that was not the case and that I was grateful for my job and pay. The reason that I applied for Amazon was to make extra money because I planned to buy a house next year. I guess he thought I might have been leaving to work for Amazon doing it but I assured him it was just a warehouse job.

He told me, "You shouldn't have to work a second job at a warehouse an hour away....how much were you planning on making? How about I let you work extra hours for us and we will pay you whatever extra you intended to make?"

Of course I accepted and that has been working out great. That is just once example of having a goal and doing anything to achieve it, but getting in return more than you expected and situations like this have been happening more and more frequently with me.

Getting a house was an obsession. The way I thought about it was I had no choice but to get into a house. Then in my mind I owned the house already. Everything I did was somehow related to getting this house. I started budgeting my finances, which helped me realize that I made great money but was recklessly spending. I cut out hanging out with friends, buying alcohol, and spending money unnecessarily. I used the money I was not blowing on BS to fix my credit by paying debts, etc. Every single day every bit of free money became about getting the house, but as a result of this one goal I was changing my life, my health, my finances, etc.

Let me break it down very simply because everyone has the ability to do this. For example you are at work and you are craving this dessert, or treat, or what have you. You cannot get it now because you are busy at work, but you know after work you are going to get in your car and drive to this place and get it. In your mind it's already yours before you see it or pay for it. Right? It's already yours. So we all do this with the easy stuff, but most of us fail to do this with goals or dreams. It's not magic or luck. It is want and desire.

Look everywhere around you. Every single little thing you see now was created by someone and did not exist at one point in time. How did this thing come to exist? A thought. Nothing would exist without thoughts. So thoughts and the types of thoughts you have are critical. What are you feeding your mind? Positive or negative thoughts?

I read that the mind is a garden. You can plant a seed, and either water it and give it nutrients, or neglect it, but whatever you sow, you will reap. I changed my whole mentality, which caused me to change my environment, which then changed my condition. It was nothing magical but very simple and most of us do not operate in a way for it to benefit us.

In terms of music you are familiar with frequency. There are lows, mids, and highs, and there are frequencies that are super low or super high that we cannot hear, but that does not mean they do not exist. So what I believe is that we are surrounded by opportunity and surrounded by answers, but you cannot use them without sharpening and focusing your thoughts. A lot of people already do this but with the negative, constantly stressing, fearful worrying; and that is exactly what they attract. That is exactly what they hear and see.

Insanity is doing the same things over and over but expecting a different result. You have to change your actions, but you cannot change your actions without changing your thoughts. You have to set a goal and be as specific as possible. Who, what, when, where, and how. I did not simply say I want a house. I told myself I would move by the end of the summer and that is what happened exactly. I find this testimony to be encouraging and furthers the notion that right thinking and a positive mindset and action are so pertinent to accomplishing anything. If you do not think properly you will not hit the target you are aiming for.

One of the things I want you to experience while reading this book is a paradigm shift. The reason someone can give such a successful testimonial is because they've experienced one. In science and philosophy a paradigm is a set of concepts or thought patterns, including theories, research methods, and standards for what constitutes a legitimate contribution to a field of study. A paradigm is like a lens in a camera that you look through to see the world to draw conclusions. The lens is the information you use to come to those conclusions.

For example, a blind man walks on to a city bus and it is full of people with nowhere to sit. One man decides to get up and give this man his seat. Good deed done right? That is very nice of someone to do correct?

Well what if I told you the man who gave up his seat was the bus driver? The conclusion that you drew went from good deed to terrible idea I hope. The reason your thought on it changed was because I presented to you information that you did not know.

See if you understand this next example. How To Fix a Drug Scandal is a docuseries on Netflix that follows the story of two lab chemists' shocking crimes that bring a state's judicial system to its knees and compromises the lines of justice for lawyers, officials, and thousands of inmates. The state where these crimes took place was Massachusetts and the revelation of this story sent shockwaves through the justice system, but it was quickly forgotten in the mainstream news. The Netflix original primarily follows the stories of Sonja Farak and Annie Dookhan. Sonja was a drug lab chemist who was arrested in 2013. Sonja worked at a crime drug lab and she let temptation get the best of her while working alone in this environment. She had access to an abundance of liquid methamphetamine. To give herself a pick-me-up as she would call it, she would sample a few drops by mouth or even put it in her soft drinks. Sonja became so addicted she would regularly take breaks just to smoke crack in order to ease her cravings. Sonja did all this while executing drug lab tests in which the results would literally dictate whether someone went to jail or not.

Annie Dookhan was a top state lab chemist who formerly worked as a chemist at the Massachusetts Department of Public Health drug abuse lab. She is now a convicted felon. She was deemed a top chemist for her uncanny ability to test drug samples four times faster than the next best chemist. No one ever questioned or looked into how she was able to work so quickly and efficiently. Through following some suspicious leads, and after being pressed by law enforcement, Annie confessed to the police that she had been "dry labbing" and falsifying criminal evidence. In a nutshell, let us say Annie received four criminal cases to sample; if they were all around the same size she would test one and if it came back positive she would sign off on all four different cases as positive results. This means she signed off on a cocaine sample that was actually table salt or powdered sugar.

Between Sonja and Annie, the falsifications affected more than fifty thousand cases. Tens of thousands of cases had to be dismissed. Tens of thousands of files had to be shredded because of the criminal actions of these two women. As a result of this revelation, men who were seen as criminals were all of a sudden exonerated free men. Records had to be expunged because the integrity of the information given to courts was devalued by the likes of a drug addict and a liar.

This is exactly what I want for you as you read through the pages of this book. I will present you the right information through scripture, personal anecdotes, and observations I make in such a way that it can free you from the prison-like cycle in which you feel trapped. What this book is NOT is a "secret" formula to getting whatever you want out of life. This book is to better help you cooperate with God's purpose and how you can play a part in it. When the conclusion is different, the action taken from that conclusion is also different. This is a paradigm shift and this is the number one takeaway I want you to have from this book. The principles presented to you between the covers of this book will make you see your life experience differently. You should no longer look back over your life and hang your head down because all of your experiences now are preparing you for the challenges ahead of you.

Many people have such a negative outlook on their circumstances. They think, "When I have this car, or this job, or this amount of money, a husband or wife, then I'll be happy." People with a negative mindset will always be unhappy and discontent no matter the results. A thermostat is a device that senses the temperature of an environment and performs actions so that the environment's temperature is maintained near a desired set point. If you have air conditioning in your bedroom set to sixty-five degrees, and the weather outside is eighty degrees, even if you crack open a window to let the warm air in, a strong thermostat system will keep the room at sixty-five degrees. Your paradigm is the temperature to which the thermostat of your mind is set. If you always have a negative attitude about your life circumstances, no good thing will change that attitude and you will always end up with the same results: angry, alone, unhappy, broke, and always negative. If the temperature of your mind is set to a cold thirty degrees, no independent heat source will ultimately change the temperature. It may get warm for a while, but eventually the thermostat will always adjust to what it is programmed to do.

This book is designed to change the thermostat setting in your mind, to shift from cold to hot, negative to positive, hopeless to hopeful, and more importantly, prison-like life cycles to destiny manifestation.

Chapter 2

Training Wheels

One of my fondest memories as a kid growing up in the West End of Providence is the first time I rode my bike without training wheels. I was five years old. It was around five o'clock. As was my custom on most days, I was waiting for my father to get home from work. We had a long driveway and big backyard. I was riding my bike adorned with training wheels. As I was riding in circles, I saw my next-door neighbor Mr. Albert come out from his garage. He spent most days working on cars. Mr. Albert had an olive-skinned face and hands stained black with oil. Although he was tall and muscular with a surly appearance, he was a very pleasant man.

"Hi Mr. Albert!" I shouted.

Ignoring my salutation, he asked, "Why you got training wheels on that bike?"

Sheepishly I retorted, "Because I cannot ride without them."

Vexed by my lack of confidence he said, "Yes you can! How old are you?"

"I am only five," I replied.

Incredulous he exclaimed, "Gimme that bike!" Along with other mumbled words.

It was as if I offended him.

I rode over to the fence. The giant man reached down with one arm, lifting my bike as if it were a toy, and brought it to his side. He walked into his garage where his museum of tools was. Fearful and fascinated at the same time, I watched as he doctored my recreational device and listened to the rhythmic clicks of the ratchet loosening the nuts on the apparent wheels to my comfort zone. Having removed them, he handed the bike back to me and said sternly, "You get back on that bike and you ride it."

What was I to do? I was afraid of falling but feared his thunderous voice even more. I reluctantly obeyed, and to my surprise I was balanced and riding smoothly. I was even able to lean into the turns when I rode fast. I could not believe it.

I yelled loudly as I rode, "I can do it!"

I knew my mother was watching from the second floor window. Elated I called out, "Mom look!!! I am riding with no training wheels!"

Typical of a Haitian mother, she looked down,

decidedly unimpressed by my new feat. I, on the other hand, was beside myself.

"Thank you Mr. Albert!" I cried out.

Having completed his task he cracked a faint smile and walked back into his sanctuary garage. I could not wait to show my dad. It's something I will never forget.

Unbeknownst to me, Mr. Albert had been watching me. Thankfully he possessed enough insight to see that the devices attached to my bike, although meant to help me, were now beneath me. They were holding me back. Often other people can see things in you that you cannot even see in yourself. You spend your whole life on training wheels thinking you cannot do something when in reality you can. I think we all have people around us who are annoyed with us, not because they dislike us, but because we tend to operate at a lower level than we should, all because we are afraid to take the training wheels off. Do not sell yourself short. Believe in your ability. There is no shame in having trouble doing that, but I hope you have people around you like Mr. Albert that can see your training wheels and have enough boldness to confront you and tell you to take them off.

One of the biggest takeaways from this childhood memory and what I want you to walk away with is this: What enables you in one season of life can be a point of hindrance in the next. I had gotten so comfortable in the state I was in that I failed to realize that I had already outgrown training wheels. I reached a point where they were not actually helping me anymore. At every life checkpoint, a survey should be taken on what to keep and what to let go because as you grow, some things will need to be shed. Are there friendships you are connected to that need to end? Are there relationships you are tied to that need to be cut off? Is your method of business losing momentum? All these questions need to be asked to begin the process of moving forward. This applies to any avenue of life, whether it be friendships, relationships, or business ventures. Applying this principle is necessary for your progression.

TAKE OFF THE LIMITS

Mr. Albert asked me a poignant question as he watched me. He asked me why I had training wheels on my bike. I could've answered in many different ways. Maybe I never thought to have them taken off. Perhaps I was enjoying my ride so much it never crossed my mind, but my answer clearly revealed the writing on the walls of my thought life: "I am only five."

Instantly that placed the barrier that was going to keep me from moving forward. My answer said my age was the basis on which I could achieve something.

My answer denoted that I had to be a certain age in order to accomplish a goal. Why did I answer that way? Even if I had never previously thought about taking my training wheels off, the response that came out of my mouth revealed the truth of what I believed. It may not have been a limitation before but after I spoke it, it put up a wall in front of me. Did I really have to be older than five years old to ride without training wheels?

Ask yourself if the things you tell yourself are true. Do you have to have a college degree to be successful? Are you really too old to enroll at a university or start a business? The conversations that you have with yourself and the people around you can very well reveal what you think about yourself and your chances at being successful in life. Begin to take a mental audit of the things you say to see if the claim you are making is actually true.

Cable business news network CNBC recently ranked the state of Rhode Island dead last in its annual listing of business climates in the United States.

Any impressionable person who is easily discouraged and thrives on negativity would use this as an excuse as to why they have not started a business or why their business is not doing well. This statistic now becomes their truth, but the actual truth is that opportunities are always there for those who make them and not for those who are waiting for one. If you allow your thoughts to be influenced by the general consensus, opportunities will never seem apparent to you, but if you keep your mind uncorrupted by what the facts tell you, opportunities are everywhere no matter the circumstance.

The Great Recession was an epoch of economic decline in the world markets in the late 2000s. Some regard it as the biggest financial meltdown since the Great Depression in the 1920s. The Great Recession stemmed from the real estate market collapse in 2007-2008. I will not go into detail but let us just say things got really bad, really quick. I remember this climate back in my early twenties. It was the end-all be-all excuse for why someone's situation was not working out the way they wanted.

"I cannot find a job because of the recession."

"I cannot put gas in my car because of the recession."

"My marriage is not working because of the recession."

Virtually everything was blamed on the recession and had it not been the recession the excuse would've been something else, yet those who chose not to let that hold them back were able to capitalize on the slump. Netflix, Amazon, and Groupon are great examples of this.

Netflix

Right now they are the internet streaming juggernaut of the world, but Netflix had humble beginnings as a DVD-by-mail service in the mid-2000s. When the recession hit, many entertainment companies went into panic mode, trying to figure out ways to withstand it.

Netflix, however, planted its feet into a nice groove and their subscriber statistics ascended. In a recession, spending eleven dollars for a movie ticket, plus another ten for a snack and another four for a soft drink or bottled water, did not seem too appealing to consumers. If you were on a date, double those prices, and if you were out with your family, quadruple that price. Hitting the movie theatre to see a box office smash hit was not very palatable in that time, especially if patrons felt like they had to take out a loan to have a great cinema experience. Waiting for it to come out on DVD sounded like a better idea. Perhaps this is where the slang 'Netflix and Chill' was born.

Netflix's success was also rooted in the fact that they

became the alternative to cable and satellite services that were relatively more expensive for consumers. People preferred paying a fraction of the cost for pretty much the same entertainment. The only difference was the methodical approach to watching your favorite programs and movies. Netflix added three million more subscribers by the end of 2009 and its stock price rose by fifty-seven percent.

Amazon

While retail companies took a big hit during the economic decline, Amazon sales rose twenty-five percent. Why? Because the folks at Amazon were shrewd businessmen and women, almost diabolical to an extent. Amazon made sure they were the top sellers for almost any product they put on their site. For example, if they saw that a particular company was the top seller in baby diapers they would first offer to buy out the company, and if that company declined, Amazon would then begin selling diapers at a lower price. This tactic would literally choke out the competition to thousands of different products. While Amazon was excellent in commerce, they always made profitability a secondary priority to customer service and competitive dominance.

Groupon

Companies that withstood the negative effects of the recession had excellent core structures that they had built upon in the years leading up to the decline, but it was not so for Groupon. They took off in the middle off the economic storm in November 2008 when their business gained revenue with thirty-five different companies. It made so much sense for consumers to utilize their services. It gave people access to what they normally would ignore during the recession. Massages are a luxury, but with Groupon they became attainable for the average person. Four-day getaways are unreachable in a plummeting economic climate, but they became affordable with Groupon. They saw much success in the midst of decline. They later turned down a six billion dollar buyout offer from Google.

You can thrive in the most difficult of situations. It's very possible. Someone may say, "Well, I am not Amazon or Netflix." They may feel as though they have to be a big name company for this to work for them but the proper principles applied to any situation can yield positive results. Limitations are meant to be surpassed. People that allow present circumstances to take precedent over the task they seek to accomplish will never hit the target of success. Training wheels will always remain attached to mediocrity. They will let age tell them it's too late to start college. They will say that the current state of affairs is not conducive to starting a business. Disregard this! Break those limits. A strong calculated plan will take hard work but will eventually lead to favorable results.

Three Take Aways

1. *Fill a need, even one that people do not know they need*
2. *Be the alternative*
3. *Look for new opportunities*

Whether it be a business, nonprofit organization, or product innovation, here are three takeaways for thriving in general or even during widespread economic hardship.

1. Fill A Need, Even One That People Do Not Know They Need

One of the keys to shifting from dream to reality is being in touch with what people need. It's about moving from knowing what they currently need to anticipating solutions to what they will need, even if they do not know they need it.

The first camera phones were released in the US in the early 2000s. By 2006 camera phones surpassed stand-alone film cameras in sales. Currently cellphones have cameras as a default feature. Before the turn of the twenty-first century, no one ever thought that a phone and a camera would go hand in hand, let alone a GPS, alarm clock, compass, entertainment device, etc., but someone saw fit to merge these two concepts and the end result has impacted culture so much. Fill a need, or even better fill a need that people never knew they needed and watch the magic happen.

2. Be the Alternative

Whether it's a recession or prosperous times, people are always looking for a bargain. People do not mind cutting off a product if it saves them a buck or two. Uber was started in 2009 by Garrett Camp and Travis Kalanick under the name UberCab. Before its inception, Camp had recently spent eight hundred dollars hiring a private car to transport him and his friends on New Year's Eve, and he was trying to figure out a way he could make the service more affordable to the average person.

Camp reasoned that allowing multiple people to share the cost of the service would drive it down, and UberCab was born.

When the company took off it started to impinge on the business of traditional taxi companies and at one point took twenty-five percent of them out of business. The cost of an Uber made much more sense to consumers than paying higher prices to a taxi company.

Uber was the alternative and now they are the mainstream. Uber operates in three hundred cities on six continents, and in 2016 grossed twenty billion.

What's even more amazing about their accomplishments is the fact that they did not own any vehicles until recently. Their only creation was an app itself and the rest involved people. Uber is a car service and the Camp/Kalanick duo did not allow the lack of vehicle ownership to limit their idea. They now sit at the top of the ride sharing industry all because they became the alternative and now they are the premium.

3. Look For New Opportunities

Evan Williams cofounded Pyra Labs to make project management software. Blogger was a note-taking feature that was a spinoff from their original plan. It was one of the first web applications for creating and managing weblogs. Williams came up with the name "blogger" and was vital in making the term "blog" such a popular and common term in modern times. Pyra Labs was acquired by Google in 2003 after some time and setbacks. Evan left Google a year later to cofound a podcast company called Odeo. With other employees from Odeo he cofounded Obvious Corporation.

Sometime after doing this iTunes moved into podcasting and dominated that market. Williams was left at a standstill, but one of Obvious Corporation's many projects was something called Twitter, a free social networking and micro-blogging service. With his original plans failing in podcasting, Evan did not fold. He sought to pave another path for success and invested in this project.

The location of the company's startup is critical. It happened in California. After a small earthquake in San Francisco, Twitter saw a surge in registrations to the site because people were documenting what they were experiencing during the shifting of tectonic plates. Evan Williams is a great example of someone who continuously and perpetually showed that in the middle of difficulty lies opportunity.

Sony's Missed Opportunity

From the early 80's to about the end of the twentieth century, Sony was the business giant when it came to portable music. The Sony Walkman was a staple in pop culture for a long time. If you had a Walkman, you were the envy of all other students at your school.

The idea for the Walkman came about when one of Sony's founders, Masaru Ibuka, pressed his engineers to make him something easier to carry. At the time he would often ride the train and use Sony's first personal cassette player called the TC-D5, which came out in 1978. It was about four pounds, cost a thousand dollars, (about four thousand at 2019 inflation levels) and was not the greatest thing to carry around. Masaru wanted something that was more conducive for daily use. Hardware engineers at Sony worked until they came up with the Sony Walkman. Masaru used it and thought the company should make it available to the public. Very few in his business camp thought this would be successful, but he pressed for it anyway.

Upon release in the United States, it took the public by storm. The Walkman brought about the dominance of the cassette over vinyl for the first time in history. "Walkman" was even added to the Oxford dictionary. The Walkman had such an impact on the culture that researchers reported a thirty percent increase in running and jogging in some form around the same time that Walkman sales reached their peak. The Walkman transitioned well when technology advanced from cassette to CD, but their demise in portable music was soon approaching.

Sony was such a powerhouse in the music realm that nothing seemed to come close to dethroning them…until the digital age revealed itself. Flash memory, MP3, and the eventual introduction of iTunes via internet all contributed to the fall of Sony in portable music. What Sony majored in was hardware, and that was key to their success in the season they were going through, but software and the digital age were on the horizon and they failed to ride that wave of progression. While digital music was first being introduced Sony developed MD, "mini disc," which was innovative because it was smaller than a CD and could hold more memory, but it was miles behind the coming digital change. At the peak time for compact discs, customers had literal folders full of hundreds of CDs. On the digital horizon you could hold all that music on one device and fit it in your pocket. Hardware was Sony's forte, but while their abundance of hardware engineers catapulted them forward in one season, it held them back in the next one. Sony's worst mistake was that they failed to ride the wave of the digital technological innovation.

The nail in the coffin was the introduction of the Apple iPod. With its vast portfolio of music and strong foundation in electronics, Sony had the arsenal to manufacture a version of the iPod way before Apple introduced it at the turn of the twenty-first century. Sony co-founder Akio Morita envisioned since the inception of the Walkman merging digital technology with media content for a new birth in user experience, but it never happened. They failed to adapt to the shift.

Initially Sony hardware engineers fought against the company's media division. Then Sony battled with how to build a device that let customers download and copy music without diminishing music sales or contracts with artists. Sony took the road less traveled and while that may be noble, it cost them so much. Their early digital music players were incompatible with the popular MP3 format. (Do Napster and Limewire ring a bell?)

After an abysmal plummet in sales, Sony pulled the noose on its "answer" to Apple's iTunes, the Sony Connect online store, after only three years. Rich Dad, Poor Dad author, Robert Kiyosaki, penned this quote in his book that is so relevant to this situation, "There is always another wave. People who hurry and catch a wave late usually are the ones to wipe out." Sony's obsession with hardware attributed to their triumph in the 80s and 90s, but eventually wiped them out in the new age of experiencing music on the go.

The take-away message in this is to always have your ear to the ground when it comes to change in your life. It is inevitable. You cannot be the same, think the same, and act the same if you hope to be successful in a world that does not remain the same. One of the greatest attributes of highly successful people is the ability to stay relevant. When going after something great you must be comfortable with your present way of thinking being challenged, always ready to continually learn, unlearn, and relearn your craft.

The key to remaining relevant is to always have the mindset that you are only as good as your last accomplishment. You cannot rest on your past reputation. From a business standpoint if you disappoint your consumers, they will always wonder if they should buy your next product. From a personal life perspective, as frustrating as it may seem, change is a good thing, and if you resist the ebb and flow of transition in life you will only survive and not thrive.

THE MANNA STOPPED

The biblical account of the Israelites is a story of triumph, defeat, hardship, and miraculous provision. I could give a long list of all the divine accommodations that God provided but I want to zero in on one of them. God rescued the Israelites from slavery in grand fashion by parting the Red Sea, and when they crossed they watched their oppressors drown in the rushing waters. It was an awesome moment of vindication for people who endured hundreds of years of slavery.

As they celebrated, God led them into the wilderness to refine them into the people He wanted them to be. Very soon after being in this dry desert the people's celebration of their freedom quickly went to grumbling and complaining about how they had no food or water. They did not put two and two together that the God who could split the Red Sea could surely provide them with food. That is exactly what He did.

One morning the Israelites woke up and outside their tents was this flake-like substance on the ground. God literally rained bread down from heaven to feed His people. That is not the most amazing part though. He did it and it sustained them in the wilderness for forty years. Where there was no soil or vegetation to plant food, God provided a vitamin rich delicacy to keep them strong for their passage. The Israelites did not need to plant, break soil, or water anything to get this. All they had to do was wake up in the morning and food was there.

Forty years is a long time to be spoiled with heavenly meals, but the manna was not the endgame.

This bread from heaven was not meant to be their food forever. One day they would have to step their game up when they were ready.

After forty years of failure, victory, and correction, the Israelites arrived to Gilgal, which is right outside the Promised Land. When they arrived, along with the daily manna they always have, they ate from the fruit of the land. The day after they ate from the fruit of the land, the manna stopped. I could imagine the low-key panic the Israelites experienced when something they had for so long was all of a sudden not there anymore. This stoppage of easy access to food could have come as a bit of a shock, but it had a purpose. It was to mark a new horizon that the Israelites were entering into. What sustained them in one season would not be available to them in the next season. It's not that the manna was bad; it was great for them, but it was not conducive to where they were going.

This goes to show that a great thing in the wrong season can be an absolutely terrible thing. God told the Israelites that the Promised Land was a land flowing with milk and honey, but it did not mean that milk and honey would flow without work. The Israelites were going to have to learn a new skill: agriculture. Agriculture is great, but in the wrong season would have been a waste of time. The Israelites were continuously on the move in the desert so planting and waiting for harvest would have been counterproductive to their objective of trying to reach Canaan. They came into new land and would not have to plant for a year because their enemies had planted already, but they would need to learn new skills in growing, sustaining, and storing food to maintain the new land they were in.

Every next level of your life will require a new and different you. Be careful not to take old habits, ways, and methods into a new place or season. Training wheels are only good for so long. At a certain point Sony should have eaten the fruit of the land of the digital age, but they sat on their hands and resisted the change that was inevitable.

The transition that you see happening in front of you is not a ruse. Do not miss the shift.

Transitions are more often than not a sign of growth, but they can bring feelings of loss. Take heart, because to get somewhere new you will have to leave certain things behind.

Chapter 3
Hunger

THE VILLAGE PEOPLE

In 2004, movie writer and director M. Night Shyamalan produced arguably what some call a masterpiece (others call it a flop) of a film called The Village. The psychological suspense thriller seems to be set in the nineteenth century following a community of people who live a simple life, but also live in fear of creatures who live in the woods beyond the village. Tactical measures are taken so that no one in the village travels beyond its boundaries and no one on the outside can break the ranks of this community. All matters and decisions are run through a board of elders who manage all important issues that affect the community. As the film progresses it is apparent that all the elders have one thing in common: They have all experienced devastating trauma in their past.

Through a series of unfortunate events a member of the community named Lucius is injured in an attack and a woman named Ivy who is in love with him seeks desperately to save him, but needs the proper medicine to do so. Due to limited resources, after pleading with the elders they allow Ivy to venture into the woods to a nearby town in order to retrieve the medicine that can save Lucius. Here's where the dilemma rears its ugly head. Ivy, the woman who desperately wants to save the love of her life…is blind.

As impossible as it sounds, Ivy boldly enters the woods and even has an encounter with the creature and outsmarts him. This is amazing; the only person with enough guts to venture outside the limits of the environment was a blind person. Handicaps are not a good excuse to not do something. Not having the drive is the reason.

Ivy continues her journey and after some time hits a literal wall, a vine-ridden fence like structure to be more accurate. She climbs it and makes her way over. To the surprise of the audience watching this film, as she makes it over the viney barrier a vehicle pulls up to confront her. The man driving the car has no idea why a woman in nineteenth century clothing is climbing over the fence of the wildlife reserve for which he works. The man driving the vehicle is a park ranger. The vehicle he is driving is not nineteenth century styled. It is very much present day modern. The big twist is this movie, which M. Night is known for, is it's not set in the nineteenth century at all. It is actually present day.

The trauma that all the elders experienced caused them all to agree to move into this wildlife reserve. They all met each other through a grief counseling center after their traumatic experiences. For twenty-plus years they have built their lives and families within the confines of this village. Not wanting to further deal with the menaces of society they enclosed themselves within this wildlife reserve to avoid any and every aspect of the outside world.

I find that to progress, you must be like Ivy and push the barriers of your normal surroundings. If you want to do things you have never done, see things you have never seen before, you must go places you have never been. Playing it safe will yield mediocre results. Often if you come from a small state or a small town the "village mentality" is infectious and beckons you to remain comfortable. I can speak on this with confidence because I come from a small city in literally the smallest state in the union. Rhode Island is the epitome of a comfort zone. Where you live, the people you hang around, those same familiar places, while comforting, could be the viney wall impeding your progress to next level places.

People with village mentality will try and keep you from moving forward by trying to discourage you. Like the elders, they will give an assortment of reasons why what you plan to do will never work. Some will encourage you outwardly but have no confidence in what you set out to accomplish inwardly. While villagers may be sincere, the ramifications of their ways are averse to your destiny.

Once identified, monitor the time you spend with

villagers. The more time you spend around them the more chance they have to indoctrinate you with their methods and thought process. Villagers will infect the dream you long to manifest. Be careful because villagers may try and draw you back into their circles by saying things like, "You do not hang out with us as much as you used too, you think you are better than us, you are too good for us now?"

What dawned on me years after seeing this movie is that in general there is always a villain and a hero in a story. Ivy is the clear "shero" of this film but who or what are the villains? While I have spoiled most of this movie for you I will not elaborate on other details. It took some thought, but the villains are the elders, the masterminds of this whole operation. Their intentions were noble, but their method was sinister. Under the guise of trying to protect their own, the elders weaved a web of deception in order to maintain their precious safe haven.

Some of the most evil things done in this world are birthed from good intentions. Never let anyone's good intentions for you be the influence or foundation for the destiny that you choose. Growing up and being raised by Haitian immigrants identifies so well with this predicament. From the time I was young, the notion that I needed to go to college and become a doctor, lawyer, nurse, or engineer was drilled into me and all my peers. I was made to believe that I would be happy if I did this If my parents were happy, then I would be happy.

I pressed my way through school thinking I chose something that suited me, but when I arrived at my destination, I was not fulfilled. I was not a master of the craft that I chose. It weighed heavily on me for so long because I had put so much work into this objective but it was not yielding the emotional, spiritual, or even financial results that I wanted. Everything became about maintaining the image that my parents wanted for me and not what I wanted for me.

One way or another you are going to have to take a leap of faith from the place that you are to the place that you want to be. The scary thing is, like Ivy, you are blindly walking into a wilderness for which you have no GPS. One of the attributes I love about Ivy is her handicap. Despite all the factors against her, the handicap of blindness alone should have been the Achilles heel to her mission, but she went anyway.

We are too often averted from our target because of what we see with our eyes. False logic will say, "Do not venture into the woods of the unknown. Stay home where it's safe." What many fail to realize is that a disability, handicap, or weakness can very well be an advantage if you perceive it correctly. Had Ivy been able to see, her fearful encounter with the creature in the woods would have further crippled her into giving up and going back home, but because she was blind, it freed her from the horror of what was chasing after her. She relied more on her other senses to outsmart her adversary. No handicap should keep you from reaching the destination that is purposed in you.

Handicaps will also cause opponents to underestimate you. Causing your opponents to mindfully place themselves in a state of comfort can lull them into a voluntary submission. Your handicap makes them feel as though maximum effort is not needed to defeat you, and so it becomes a strength for you and a weakness for them. A visible weakness in yourself can grow arrogance in your enemy. Do not despise your perceived weakness. It may launch you into a place of success.

ADVANTAGE OF A DISABILITY

I had an interesting conversation with a former professional MMA fighter in 2019. He retired around the time CEO Dana White was given the reins over the UFC. I was taken aback when he told me he was born with a degenerative muscle disease which caused partial blindness in him. I asked him how it came about that he became a mixed martial artist. He said when he was younger he could not go to school. There was no home school available for him as a child, so he was enrolled into karate classes. Fast forward to his adult life, karate was all he knew.

Vision is such an important factor in fighting so I asked him how he was able to maneuver through combat. He told me flying fists were difficult to see, but from a young age he was taught to always watch hip movement. Just like dancing, in fighting, the hips tell the story. The hips must rotate a certain way to throw a certain punch. He was taught not to watch his opponents so much in the eyes, but to focus more on their center of mass. Because of his disadvantage he was forced to really learn and become accustomed to hip movement. He had to be sharper than average to capitalize on his opponents to get the win.

I then asked if his opponents knew about his degenerative muscle disease. He said yes. This also was an advantage for him, he said, because he often felt some laxity in his opponents. They did not take him as seriously as they would a fighter without such a handicap because they did not think a certain level of intensity was necessary, but after a round with him in the octagon it was clear to them that he was not to be taken lightly. While he was not a UFC champion, he saw victory in many matches because he knew how to flip his disadvantage into an advantage. This is key to attaining excellence.

Disadvantages are inevitable. You are going to have them no matter how sharp you think you are. The important thing is perspective. You must own it. You must embrace imperfection to move past it and desire what's ahead of you.

They that desire much must be hungry. For my thirtieth birthday my wife took me out to eat. It's customary for me that I request a gift and a nice dinner at a restaurant. This particular year my wife Charlene took me to a place called *The Nordic Lodge*. It was a buffet restaurant, but this was no ordinary run-of-the-mill buffet. Normally it costs anywhere from twenty to thirty dollars to go, but this buffet was different. It cost one hundred dollars per person to get in and you had two hours to eat whatever you like. There was lobster, steak, scallops, jumbo crab, ribs, etc. They had it all.

It's important that you are around people who have a buffet mentality. People with a buffet mentality want all they can eat for the time they have on this earth. When my wife paid the admission to the Nordic Lodge, the host showed us to our table. Once we sat down and placed our belongings, we did not wait to be served. We grabbed our plates and headed towards the food. Too often we sit down in life and wait to be served when in reality you must go and get it for yourself. You make your choices. You can never blame someone else for what you put on your own plate.

Different levels of hunger can often breed contempt between people. When you are striving for more out of life people will look at you and say that you are arrogant, a know-it-all, and a show-off. Vice versa, you will look at those with no hunger and think they are lazy, mediocre, and underachieving.

A great way to stay hungry is to follow or, even better, be around people who do what you do better than you. As a matter of fact, when you are in a room full of people who operate at a higher level than you, the best thing to do is shut up. Do not talk too much; listen more and ask questions when opportunities present themselves. That way you can absorb as much as you can from the environment and the people around you. You can essentially eat off of everyone's plate around you. Do not try to be a show off, especially when you are in a room full of greatness. Your immaturity and lack of tact will be apparent to everyone in the room and some will even be bold enough to put you in your place. Hold on to your humility.

When you are invited somewhere distinguished, never sit down in the best place. Jesus teaches us in Luke, Chapter 14, that when someone of more honor shows up, the host who invited you will ask you to move and give up your spot to the person with more honor. Always take the lowest place, play your position, and when the time comes the host will tell you to go higher. You will then be elevated in the presence of esteemed people.

I played the drums growing up and it was something I loved to do. There were times I would become lax in my effort to learn new techniques and concepts but there was one surefire way to reignite my appetite for excellence, and that was watching someone do what I do at a higher level. Watching their speed, technique, and style would make me look at my own skill level and think, "Man, I am nothing. I am never playing drums again." While that may be a general sentiment of most young musicians when they hear someone perform at a high level, it makes us go back to our respective training grounds to hone our craft. Whether you are a concert pianist, nuclear physicist, public speaker, or entrepreneur and you want to stay hungry, go watch someone do what you do at a high level and when they blow you away with their skill, you go back home and work on yours.

Another great way to stay hungry is to always be mindful of the Law of Diminishing Intent. This law was coined by American entrepreneur Jim Rohn and it states, "The longer you wait to do something you should do now, the greater the odds that you will never actually do it." Wise author and Pastor John Maxwell piggybacks off this and says, "One of these days, turns into none of these days." At the point of inspiration you must act on it in order to continue on your path to success. If a great idea comes to you, do not put it off for tomorrow or some future occurrence. Do it now. If you are a writer and an idea comes to you, write it down now. Put it in your phone. If you are in film production and you get an idea for a short film, make a call to your screenwriter about what you want to do. You always want your first move to set off a chain of events for the next. Your path through progress will flow with each action you take. Does life get in the way? Most definitely, but you must be devoted to keep moving.

I heard a story of a father who told a riddle to his son. Five frogs are sitting on a log. Four decide to jump off. How many are left? Any normal person's kneejerk response would be one, but that is incorrect. The answer is five. Why? Because there is a world of difference between deciding to do something and actually doing something. Down to even the most practical things, do not be at the mercy of this law. You will miss deadlines, you will be late and your dream, business, or aspiration will suffer the negative consequences. Many people fall subject to The Law of Diminishing Intent, but it can be countered with continuous action that is powered by hunger. To hunger is to continuously strive for everyday progression.

If there is something you love to do, whatever it may be, understand that there is no final destination, but it is a continuous journey. Even in the academic realm it's apparent in the language they use to denote someone's completion of a graduate program. At whatever level you finish you receive a degree; Bachelors, Masters, or Doctorate. What you have not done is attained all there is to know about that field of study. You only know it to a certain degree. You should feel that way about everything in which you find meaning. You should always be hungry to know more about whatever you devote yourself to and find fulfillment. Primarily it should be God, but it could be music, film, writing, mathematics or even with someone you are in a relationship. The more satisfied you feel about it the less hunger you will have and the less hunger you have, the less drive you will feel towards it. The key to remaining hungry is to always cling to the mindset, "I have not begun to learn. There is much more to discover."

There is an appetite for destiny and if you do not have one it can be awakened. Appetite dictates the direction of your life. Appetite dictates how far in your destiny you can go. When the Israelites were in the wilderness in the Book of Numbers after escaping Egypt, God brought them to the edge of the Promised Land and sent twelve spies in to survey the land. They went in and brought out some of the fruit that grew in the land. They also brought a report of who they saw. They ate the fruit of the land of promise. They loved the food but when they heard the negative report of the giants that inhabited the land, they refused to enter into what God had for them. They lost their appetite and because of this it caused them to wander in the wilderness for forty years.

Do not let fear of fighting to get where you are

supposed to be kill the desire you have inside you. If you do not hunger for the right things it will constantly cause you to repeat certain things in your life. You will leave one nine-to-five job because you are unhappy only to find another nine-to-five and be just as miserable. You will leave one boyfriend / girlfriend and find another only to realize they have the same problem as the last. Maybe you are not supposed to work a regular nine-to-five job. Maybe the type of girl or guy you have been going after is not the right type for you.

You must understand that when you make a decision to follow wholeheartedly after God's purpose for your life, your appetite may have to change. You cannot continue to desire the old things when you are in a new place. When the Israelites were slaves in Egypt, they were accustomed to a certain type of diet. Under Egyptian oppression they were used to eating fish, garlic, and onion. After God freed them and sent them into the wilderness they often complained that they desired the food they used to eat when they were under Pharaoh. They would often reach a point of desperation in the wilderness, and instead of trusting God to provide for them like He had done repeatedly, they would groan and complain for what they used to have.

Their time in the wilderness was not in vain however. God was using this time to change their appetite so they would be ready for the new food they would eat in the Promised Land. When you are venturing into new territory you must be ready for an appetite change. Clinging to old desires will only keep you from moving further into the new horizon.

I often use athletes as an example of this because literally overnight you can go from having nothing to being a multi-millionaire. Michael Vick is a great example of improper appetite. He was a premiere player coming out of Virginia Tech and was drafted by the Atlanta Falcons. After playing very well and proving himself, he was at one point the highest paid player in the NFL. He was on top of the world until reports of him being involved in an illegal dog fighting ring surfaced in the media. Further investigations were made and the truth that followed was ugly. His reputation quickly plummeted and the news put his football career on life support. Michael could have gone further into his destiny as an athlete but he allowed improper appetite to direct his decisions. Where Michael Vick was from, dog fighting was very common. He did not see much wrong with it because that was the lifestyle he was used to, but he failed to make the shift in his appetite when he went from a no-name athlete to a nationally known phenomenon. Vick took an old appetite into a new place and it nearly ruined him.

The mistake that the Israelites made was, when they got near the Promised Land in the Book of Numbers, they treated it like it was a sample instead of an appetizer. What is a sample? A sample is like when you go to the supermarket or wholesale club and there are people who are there at stands who do not work for the market, but are trying to give you a taste of something. Once you have a taste you cannot have more unless you decide to buy, you can leave and keep going.

An appetizer, however, is something that a chef gives you in order to whet your appetite. It would be foolish for you to leave the appetizer because it is not the end. The chef has something more for you to have.

Many of you have gotten a taste of what God has for you and you have treated it like a sample and for whatever reason, whether it be fear or procrastination, left, but if you hunger for more the Chef in heaven has something greater cooking for you. There is more to life than just the mundane routine you do week to week. You cannot just want it. You must want more of it. Where is your hunger? Why have you become satisfied with the way things are? Why have you settled for just salad? Salad Faith yields salad results. You have to believe God for something big if you want to see something big. You have to believe God for something big if you want to experience something big. If you do not have the right hunger you will travel in circles, never receiving that which belongs to you.

There are things inside of you that God has placed there that will die there if you do not cooperate with Him. Cemeteries are full of dead dreams, destinies, and accomplishments that could have been realized in the people that are buried six feet under the foundation of every tombstone.

Do not be fooled though; while it may die with you it, does not mean the destiny will not be accomplished. It will be done by someone else. God is not sitting in heaven heartbroken over whoever does not want to cooperate with his divine will. He can always find someone else to do what

He wants on this Earth. God can find someone drunk and high on cocaine sleeping under a bridge, who will out sing, dance, preach, engineer, doctor, degree, and accomplish you so His divine exploits can be realized.

God made an example out of a whole generation of people by not allowing them to enter the Promised Land. They refused to get on board with what He had planned for them. While the journey was difficult all they had to do was remain faithful to Him and God would see them through any bit of adversity, but what they did was complain, murmur, and reject the very plan that was going to elevate them and ultimately bring God glory.

We have to remember that your worst enemy in this life is yourself sometimes. We complain and are bitter with the cards that we've been dealt in this life. This is not the proper reaction to have. Adversity you face on a regular basis can leave you drained and hopeless sometimes but when you have the right perspective it should drive you to remain steadfast and faithful to God's plan. You will find that some of the most triumphant parts of your life were riddled with adversity. "It was the best of times, it was the worst of times" will often be the narration to memories of victory you have had in your past.

As I wrote the pages of this book, my wife was going through an unpleasant pregnancy and my son was birthed at two pounds. He was born with a hole in his heart preventing him from breathing correctly, and his chest cavity was filling up with fluid. Doctors were hoping the hole would close, but after a month it did not, and my son continued to experience low breathing spells that required intervention from nurses to get him stable. It was very disheartening to watch them stab him with needles trying to find a vein in his tiny body. At one point doctors concluded they must operate on him and I was vehemently opposed to that notion but I understood that it was necessary. Surgery for a less-than-five-pound baby just did not make sense to me and I expressed that to God so He could intervene. The doctors said he would need to be transferred to Boston to have the surgery and the day they took him I accepted that it had to happen, but I prayed that God himself would be the surgeon in that room.

On the morning of the surgery it was routine for the doctors to do one last echocardiogram to know exactly what they were dealing with. When they checked the echo, it showed that the hole had gotten significantly smaller. When the nurses said that, I assumed the operation would still happen, but while we were waiting for more information my wife and I could hear the nurses whispering that the hole was nearly closed. Finally the nurse practitioner came into the room and said at this point it would make no sense to operate because the equipment they were going to use for the surgery was bigger than the hole in my son's heart. They cancelled the surgery. God showed up to operate before any of the doctors could. All my wife and I could do was laugh and give Him all the credit.

Traumatic pregnancy, complications with my wife and a two-pound baby boy, not to mention the coronavirus pandemic were all going on while I wrote this book and finished my certification in ministerial training. I do not say this to toot my own horn but I say this to give all credit to God and encourage you to know that all things work together for good to them that love the Lord. You can absolutely, positively accomplish whatever God has set in your heart to do. He will never set you on a path that he will not give you the grace for. If you stay faithful and hungry for the path set before you, you can see victory in whatever you do. Do not let excuses and complaints about the real adversity you see keep you from finishing strong. Psalm 23 speaks of David describing how God has prepared a feast on a table before him in the presence of his enemies. Perhaps the reason you have not seen the victory over enemies you face in life is because you refuse to sit and eat at the table that God has set for you. Stay hungry and you can triumph over whatever comes your way.

Chapter 4
Long Faith

We live in a time where technology has become very advanced and we have not even begun to see where innovations can go from here. Things can be done so quickly in this age and most of society thrives on the coattails of convenience. How things can be made easier and how much people will pay for it is the topic of discussion in boardrooms at the top of corporate buildings. The more convenient it is, the more expensive it is. In the 90s if you left home and someone wanted to call you on the phone they would have to wait until you returned to get in touch with you, but now because of the cellphone you can be reached anywhere at any time.

If you needed a ride somewhere and none of your friends were available, you would either have to walk or take the bus which takes you much longer, but now you can contact a complete stranger on Uber and they will come pick you up and drive you wherever you want to go. If you ordered something from a TV commercial, you had to wait almost a month to receive your package, but now if you have Amazon Prime you can receive something in two days and sometimes even within twenty-four hours. Google has made it possible for people to find answers to almost any question.

A whole world of information is either at our fingertips or the palm of our hand. God forbid if the website you want takes more than two seconds to fully load. I am certain you can agree that you get frustrated when the page does not load in the time you want. We've come to yearn for things so quickly that researchers have concluded that people cannot wait more than a few seconds for a video to load. Computer science professor Ramesh Sitaraman at UMASS Amherst observed the viewing tendencies of 6.7 million internet users in a study released in 2015. The study concluded that internet users were only willing to wait two seconds. Any longer than that and they moved on to the next attention grabber. After five seconds the abandonment rate was twenty-five percent and if it reached ten seconds it was fifty percent.

We live in an age where you can receive quickly and we have grown accustomed to instant gratification. This can sometimes get in the way of our walk with God and the journey to destiny because while

He is all powerful and can do what He wants, God is not in the business of getting things to you quickly. With some exception God only gives things to you when you are ready. In this faith walk with God, in order for you to become what God has purposed in you, you need long faith. You have to wait and there is no way around it.

God freed the Israelites from under the hand of Pharaoh in grand fashion. The author of Exodus lets us know early in Chapter 13: 17-22 that as they were leaving, God did not lead them by way of the Philistines along the shore of the Mediterranean which was nearer. Everybody knows that the shortest distance between two points is a straight line. This was the shortest route to Canaan, the Promised Land. If God had led the Israelites the short way they would have resolved to turn back to Egypt. If you remember who the Philistines were, they were the fiercest enemies to God's people. Their first encounter would come years later in the book of Joshua where they defeat them but not completely. It was clear that the Israelites did not have the experience or the character to handle that path because God will not take you anywhere your character cannot keep you.

There are a certain set of experiences you need to have in order to handle where you are going. God could have easily defeated the Philistines for them but his concern was more with the unprepared and fear-ridden hearts of the Israelites. What a waste it would have been for God to lead those people the shorter way, defeating the Philistines, taking down the giant walls to Canaan only to be gripped by fear and trembling when they saw the giants who lived behind those walls. They were not ready and this may be true for you too. If you feel stuck or like things are taking longer than they should it may be a sign that you are not yet ready for the destination. There are no shortcuts to success and there are none with God either. He led them the long way in order to mature them for where they were going.

A constant reminder for the people to know they would make it to where God was leading them was the bones of Joseph. In faith Joseph mentioned the coming Exodus escape and gave counsel on how he wanted his bones to be preserved. Joseph made it clear to his children that when he died he did not want to be buried in Egypt. This was done at the end of his life, which showed that God would fulfill his promise to give the Israelites the Canaan land.

It would have been easy for Joseph to tell the Israelites that Egypt was their new permanent home. Joseph was the second most powerful man in arguably one of the strongest empires in the world. Secure in his position, he could have coerced his brothers to stay, but to encourage the Israelites to stay in Egypt would have shown disbelief in the promises of God. Despite his wealth, status, and power, Joseph was an outsider. He was a Hebrew among Egyptians. They were a despised people and even though powerful he would always be seen as less in their eyes. It's important to know that comfort should never be a reason to remain in a place of complacency. You should always shoot for higher when you know the place that you are is not for you.

Joseph's bones were a sign of God's coming promise to the Israelites. God always keeps his promises. God foreknew that Pharaoh would turn against Israel and He would not have it any other way. God's promise was Canaan for the Israelites. He allowed their situation to get so bad that they cried out to Him to rescue them. Had things remained favorable for them in Egypt they would have stayed where they were. You will not be resolved to move on until you are sick of where you are. Many people want to blame the enemy for things that happen but it is something God allows within His sovereignty. Rebuking spirits and naming and claiming will not change the situation. One way or another God will tell you when it's time to go. If it's a job, God will cause things to be uncomfortable. If you do not listen, He'll put you in such a position that you cannot stay. He would even go as far to cause you to be fired.

Egypt was a place of paradise and refuge and Jacob's family settled in the land of Goshen by the authority of Joseph. It was a place of prosperity in the midst of famine everywhere else, but God's purpose was not for them to remain there. God's promise was Canaan so in order to get them there He made it uncomfortable for them. Had Egypt remained a pleasurable experience for them they would have stayed. In fact many times through the Exodus and the wilderness account the people complained about going back. When faced with death, they said it would have been better to die in Egypt. They pleaded with God to come out of slavery but when faced with uncertainty in the wilderness they preferred to return to hard labor because people prefer what they are used to.

As the Israelites headed out of Egypt they passed through a placed called Succoth and camped at Etham, which was right on the edge of the wilderness. You are right at the edge of a journey worth taking and you need long faith to take the leap. Israel's stop at Etham marked the incoming transition from cultivated to uncultivated land. The journey you are going on you may not know where your next meal comes from. You do not need to know. It will be provided along the way because God never sets you in a direction without the grace to endure it. You could be on the verge of something great, but if you do not step into the wilderness you will never see what is on the other side. At the outer edge of comfort is the freedom of the unknown.

The unknown scares people. People prefer the comfort of bondage rather than the uncultivated freedom of the unknown. Freedom to the Israelites may not have looked very appealing because the land they were venturing into could not take seed. This means natural resources were very limited. Israelites were to depend on God for everything. The uncultivated land of the wilderness was the image of the mind of the Israelite. They were under slavery for four hundred years and that was all they knew. God wanted to give them a new mindset so they would be ready for the Promised Land. The Israelite mind was uneducated and not prepared to be planted. This is why the shorter route would not have been beneficial to them.

Though they had to go the long way, they had a powerful advantage. The manifest presence of God led the people, and He never left them. God's presence guided them in two forms. It was a pillar of cloud by day and a pillar of fire by night. Aside from being a glorious spectacle to see this phenomenon had practical function.

The wilderness, or desert as some call it, is known to be extremely hot during the day but frigid at night. The pillar of cloud functioned as protection and shade from the heat of the sun. As long as Israel stayed under the shadow of the cloud they could endure the length of time they were in the desert. Long faith requires that you stay in close proximity to the presence of God. Long faith begs the discipline of prayer to be a primary practice in your daily life. When you are in the wilderness you have to rely on God for everything. When you are in an unfamiliar, uncultivated desert of the unknown, your decisions need to be God led.

At night God was a pillar of fire. This was a perfect manifest presence because the desert can reach frigid lows. The closer you were to the pillar the better you were. Long faith requires that you stay close to the flaming presence of God. God's presence gives you full coverage. A really good job with great pay is nothing without great health coverage. Normally that health coverage is for you in the state that you are in and nowhere else. If you were to take a vacation out of the country and you injured yourself you would not be able to use your healthcare benefits in that foreign place. The coverage may be for you but you cannot benefit from it unless you are in proximity of where the agreement was made. In this same way following the presence of God requires that you remain close to Him. Close so that you do not succumb to the frigid air of desert nights and spiritually close so that you understand what your next step will be on your journey to destiny.

The pillar of cloud and fire also acted as a GPS. Scripture says the pillar led them by day and night. Long faith requires movement. Because scripture says they were led, that makes me see that God did not move until they were ready. They moved from Succoth to Etham. Many times people are waiting for a sign to take a risk or move. You complain that you are waiting on God to tell you when to leave that job, start a business, move on from things that you are familiar with but you are not waiting on God, God is waiting on you to make a move. Long faith requires you to make moves. Israelites knew through oral history that the Promised Land was for them. God promised them that was where they were going from the beginning. They did not need any more confirmation. How much more confirmation do you need to take the leap?

As a people, when they travelled by night the pillar of fire allowed them to see only so far in front of them. In ancient times they were no streetlights. There was no illumination of architecture off into the night's distance. It was crucial to have some sort of light source to make a safe path visible. Enough light to see right in front of them made sure that they did not get ahead of God in where they were going. Be sure that when you are moving forward in what God has set for you that you are not getting ahead of yourself and Him. The most important step is the next one. That is crucial when you are in uncharted territory.

Psalm 119:105 says that God's word is a lamp to guide my feet and a light to my path. Do not get too focused on the light at the end of the tunnel when God promises to light the way that is directly in front of you. You do not know enough about the landscape you are on to make decisions that are too far ahead into the future. This can often give people anxiety and worry about what is to come because all you see is darkness, but you have to focus on what is illuminated and that is the next step in front of you. You need long faith on this journey through destiny. When you have God's approval and cosign, it does not matter how long and arduous a task is, you can absolutely make it to the end destination, but it starts with the faith of the first step.

Chapter 5
Fighting Faith

I took self-defense classes in my mid to late twenties. I participated off and on for about seven years. I have met some of the nicest people who were equipped with bone breaking deadly techniques. What I find most ironic about this experience is while they taught me aggressive techniques, the motive or foundation they instructed from was to avoid a fight at all costs. We would run drills called verbal diffusing that centered on defending and talking your way out of an altercation. If there is anything that is true to life, it is there are some fights that you should not avoid. Some fights you cannot circumvent. It is normal for us to want to take the path of least resistance in life, but on this faith walk with God there are some battles you will have to fight.

We are going to analyze the classic account of David and Goliath in Samuel Chapter 17. While the majority knows the overall gist of the story, many are not aware of the circumstances around what led to this momentous event. David was not just some puny teen who picked a fight with a ten-foot bully. He was a shepherd in his father's house. He was one of eight sons and was often forgotten due to the notion that he may have been the result of an adulterous affair. He was disregarded by his father and despised by his older brothers. Herding sheep was a job reserved for convicts and slaves but David was perfect for the job because of how his family esteemed him. David's circumstances were designed to keep him in a lowly place, but destiny could not be shut out of his situation. David did what he was told, followed orders, and this led to his elevation.

David follows his father Jesse's instructions to bring food to his brothers who are gearing up for a fierce war. His obedience puts him at the right place at the right time. In the previous chapter where this story is located, David was anointed as king of Israel. It would have been easy for him to be arrogant seeing that he was clearly mistreated by his father and brothers. David did not carry a chip on his shoulder. The only thing he carried was anointing and confidence in God. David was not consumed with bitterness and he was not going to use his newfound position to get revenge on those who mistreated him. Out of all the times David could have arrived to the battle line, he showed up right when Goliath was making his daily proclamation of insults. It was divine appointment that David heard Goliath's defiance because it incited a righteous anger within him. It was clear that every man was afraid. They did not have the boldness to confront him. When men were running away David toed the line.

Along with the big risk of fighting Goliath, there was a big reward. The king offered a large lump sum of money, his daughter's hand in marriage, and tax exemption for his entire house. Understand that pursuing a Goliath that is larger than life has a larger than life reward. Anything worth going after is going to be difficult, but the more information David received the more he inquired. David had courage and boldness which gave him a different attitude than the rest of the military. The soldiers spoke with fear but David spoke with righteous indignation. David asked what the reward was and they told him. He also insulted Goliath. More than the protracted reward from the king, David was not about to sit around while someone disrespected his God and country.

One thing that gave David his drive was that he was going for something bigger –fight. His "why" gave him the fuel to fight for something bigger than himself. His "why" gave him fuel to fight for his "what." David's "why" was the honor of his God and his country. Many times, you cannot reach your "what" because you have not discovered your "why." David's drive did not stop with him. It was for everything he loved. What are you striving for? Is there a why behind it? There must be something that wakes you up in the morning.

While David was asking questions, his brother

heard him and it made him angry. David's confidence upset his brother. Your confidence in what you do and the goal you set for yourself will often upset people around you. Truthfully speaking it's most likely your friends, family, or the people closest to you. Those who have been around you the longest are very common with you and often cannot see or dismiss the greatness in you. Some people envy the boldness that they wish they had themselves. When people see a trait in someone else they wish they had, it often creates hostility. David, however, did not devote much attention to his brother's anger. David's focus was on the main fight.

It's one thing to have fighting faith, but it's another when you are in the right fight. It's important to know that you shouldn't waste time engaging in a fight that does not mean anything or lacks a significant reward. If David was caught up bickering back and forth with his brother, he would have missed his real opportunity. Never let anyone divert your attention from the fight you are supposed to be in. No one is worth losing your temper over. Anger in a small insignificant argument will label you a fool. David was not about to be diverted by something that was a waste of his time. Goliath was the main fight so all his attention was on him. He turned his attention away from that which tried to avert him from his fight. It's very simple. When you are caught up bickering in the wrong petty quarrel, you are missing the fight you are supposed to be engaged in. David resolved to fight the right fight.

As David made his way through the military camp,

word got around to King Saul that someone was interested in fighting the giant, so he sent for him. As David walked in, Saul took one good look at him and wrote him off. He told him he was too young to fight. Matter of fact, Goliath had been trained since David's age, twelve to fifteen. Nothing could sway David from his daunting task. David had a resume. He had receipts. David stood before Saul like he was on an episode of Shark Tank and pitched his plan to kill this behemoth. David was a sheep keeper and made Saul aware of the fact that when a lion or bear came and took one of his sheep in its mouth; he grabbed it by its hair and clubbed it to death. This was not David's first rodeo and he wanted all the smoke. He knew in his heart that he could put down this champion. David was self-aware enough to know that every challenge and adversity he experienced was preparing him for where he was going. Goliath would be the first of many battles in which David engaged.

David's pitch was so good it convinced King Saul. Matter of fact Saul was willing to invest armor and weaponry in him. He dressed David in his own King's armor. Saul put his helmet on his head and girded him with his king's sword. It only took David a few steps to realize that he could not maneuver well in someone else's armor.

We often take on missions and objectives in someone else's armor and because of this we fail. It was hypocritical for Saul to force armor on someone when he would not even wear it himself. Do not let people force advice, opinions, and perspectives on you that they do not even stand on or follow themselves. Saul's helmet would've ruined David's vision. His tunic armor would've weighed David down, ruining his pace, and Saul's sword would've ruined David's method of attack. People may mean well but their advice, opinion, and perspective that they do not stand on will lead to your demise.

What's so ironic in this story is Saul known to be a "head and shoulder taller than anyone in Israel." If there was anyone that could go toe to toe with Goliath, it should have been King Saul. What's even more fascinating is Saul was from a lineage of great warriors. He was descended from the tribe of Benjamin. As a matter of fact, in Israel's biblical history an army of seven hundred men from Benjamin assembled to go to war in the Book of Judges Chapter 20:16. All seven hundred of them were left-handed stone slingers who could hit a target at a "hairsbreadth and not miss." If there was anyone to fight Goliath, it should have been Saul, but he did not have the drive, the courage, or boldness to toe the battle line. David, equipped with the Spirit of God, was the man for the job.

When you are operating in the purpose that God has set for you nothing can stand in your way. There will be disappointments and setbacks, but when you have got fighting faith you can stand the test of every challenge that comes your way. You can in fact do this, but not in anyone else's armor or with someone else's weaponry. God will not use the person you pretend to be. You have to complete your objective in your own skin, and in his own skin, David did. Armed with just five stones and a sling, David conquered Goliath with one shot. David had fighting faith to win this battle and fighting faith is all you need for a fighting chance. David's victory took him from the sheep pen to the king's palace. David had no idea that there was a shift in progress when he was simply doing what he was told. Such a small task led to an enormous win.

Do not despise small beginnings. Do everything wholeheartedly. The most mundane of tasks can lead to the greatest of opportunities. Whatever you do, do it with everything you have got. I have failed to take this advice in my past. Whenever I got weary working a job I did not like, my performance would diminish.

I remember working a job that I began to be discouraged with. I started to mimic the attitude of those around me. Doing just enough to get by, so I could punch in and punch out. I felt like my mind and intelligence could be used for much more than what I was doing. I would constantly think about this while taking home a check every week that I did not feel was enough. Instead of planning my future and shooting for more, I stayed where I was and sulked in my dissatisfaction. I began to just go through the motions, living on autopilot. I smiled when I was supposed to and swept all other feelings under the rug until the lump of dust got so big other people could see it.

Do not let the dissatisfactions of life keep you from being and doing your absolute best. Do the job you do not like, work the position you cannot stand, but when you get home, you work your dream. How senseless is it to devote forty-plus hours a week to build someone else's dream and then you go home and not build your own. Netflix, Hulu, Facebook, and Instagram will not do it for you. You are going to have to do it yourself. Goals without plans are just wishes, but if you devote yourself to a lifestyle of excellence you can manifest what you visualize in your mind.

When you have fighting faith you are never too big for small tasks. If you have a fighting chance your character will put you in rooms you have never seen before. One thing that is super important to know is your status should not dictate how well you do something. How you feel about where you are in life should not be the motivation behind how you make a living or walk in your purpose. This is a destructive way to go about life because you will experience disappointing days and if you live off of what you are feeling you will see little to no progression. It's okay to know that you do not like your current status or situation, but it should not show up in your work or how you treat people. This mindset can sabotage your future.

This example can be seen in the sports world. It's nothing new to see an amazing athlete reduced to nothing but bad news when they are facing contract issues. I am certain you have heard it before when a star quarterback sees his peers are signing multi-million dollar contracts and because he feels he is just as talented, he should be paid the same amount of money or more. The quarterback plays hard every game and he feels like that's being ignored by the team management. The player begins to give disgruntled interviews in the media. His play begins to decline. His relationship with teammates begins to deteriorate. By the end of the season he gets what he wants or the next best thing. His team releases him and he is open to sign with whatever team he wants.

What he does not realize is while he was dissatisfied with his old team, there was a spotlight on him. Every other team was watching and hearing about what he was doing. They knew about the strife he had with upper management and teammates. They saw the disgruntled interviews and he went from being a precious commodity to someone nobody wanted to deal with. Do not get too big for where you are. You may not like your job or current situation but until you are ready to leave, do your absolute best.

GET IN YOUR LANE

You will know that you are in your element when you can do more with less than others have. You have to make it your priority to find your niche. A niche is a suitable position in life where you can thrive. You cannot waste your time weighing yourself down copying things other people do to become successful. It will only be a burden to you.

In 2019 I never would have thought that a war over fried chicken could teach such a great lesson in getting and staying in your lane. Chick-fil-A has been a powerhouse in the fast food industry for years now. Not only are they known for their chicken sandwiches and great sauce, but their customer service is second to none. Low and behold, Popeye's Chicken, a lower-tiered restaurant chain, decided to challenge Chick-fil-A's chicken sandwich with their own. While the sandwich had a spicy kick, and was average in my opinion, it sent the social media world into a frenzy. There were countless videos and posts of people arguing about which sandwich was better. The war went viral.

Chick-fil-A was accustomed to long lines. Whenever their restaurant would open a new location, people would literally camp outside days before the grand opening just to be first in line to have their divine chicken. They had the personnel and the training to handle the volume of people they were serving. Popeye's on the other hand was not equipped with the same weapons. Once the chicken war started it was evident that the employees were not ready for the amount of people they had to serve, at least not consistently on the level that Chick-fil-A was. Soon people started posting videos on social media of Popeye's employees lashing out at customers, customers fighting other customers, and customers attacking Popeye's employees. No amount of spinach could help this mess.

It was pitiful to watch the digression of this establishment, but at the same time it was not shocking. Popeye's is not built like their counterpart. They did not have the personnel or the training and to top it off, the final nail in the coffin for Popeye's was they ran out of chicken. Their main supply was depleted. It really revealed who the better business was. Popeye's did not know enough to stay in their lane. Chick-fil-A knew what their lane was and stuck with it. They were not trying to sell wings like Popeye's. They were confident in what they had to offer.

In this same way you need to be settled in the things you are talented in. If you try to operate in a lane you are not built for it will leave you depleted and drained. Do not go bankrupt trying to be something you are not. It's time to start being confident and comfortable in the things you have to offer. When you find your lane and stay in it, giants come down.

If there is anything more annoying than small talk (Hello, how is everything? What have you been doing lately?), it's having to listen to people talk about everything they are going to do knowing they are all talk. They talk big but do not produce big. Take a page out David's handbook and make sure you back up your tough talk with tough moves. Faith is the substance of things hoped for, the evidence of things not seen. It's one thing to have fighting faith, but you can take it to a whole other level when you put that faith in action.

David toed the battle line and inquired about the threat that was scaring every soldier out of their gladiator boots. David went around talking tough about who was terrorizing his people, so much so that it upset his older brother Eliab who was in the army. Out of all the people to be rude, Eliab, a tall and strong soldier, chose to step against his puny little brother. How hypocritical of him to all of a sudden get a backbone when he could have used that same energy to fight Goliath.

David was not just talk; he was all about that action. He saw an opportunity and did not just talk about it amongst soldiers and King Saul. He went down to a brook and got five smooth stones to put down the giant. It did not stop there. David could have surely run away when Goliath approached him, but he did not just say what he would do to the giant; he started swinging his sling and that is exactly what you need to do. Start swinging.

Do not just talk about applying for that job. Pick up the phone and call them. Fill out an application. Do not just talk about how you plan to apply to that school. Go visit the university and speak with an admissions officer. Do not brag about how you are going to open a business. Put in the application for the LLC. The things you look to conquer will never come down unless you start swinging. Put your fighting faith into action and it will set you on a journey that God will lead.

Chapter 6
Know Thyself

Set sail out to sea. Put some bait on a fishing hook and throw the reel. It would not take long before you caught anything, especially if you are subtle, discreet, and completely undetected. Before you know it, something takes that bait and you reel in a massively naïve fish. You grab your fillet knife and cut the fish open to find bones covered with pure white meat, fresh out of salt water. Now taste it, and to your surprise, it's bitter. Not a lick of salt. How are fish able to live in a particular environment and not have specific products of that environment within them?

I can remember when I was in high school, I was fundraising for the football team and I was walking door to door selling discount gold cards. I lived in a very diverse neighborhood right on the border of Cranston and Providence. Cranston is a very suburban city where the majority of people are Caucasian. Middle to upper-middle class resides there. Providence however, is a very urban inner city. Mostly black, Spanish, and low income families live there.

I was a couple of blocks from my house on the Cranston side of town and I knocked on the door of a house. A white woman in her mid-forties answered the door. Before I could smile and say hello, she abruptly slammed the door in my face. I was confused. Did I do something wrong? I laughed and thought to myself, this must be the first time a black person knocked on her door because clearly she was frightened. Not to mention that I was in the sun all day, double session football practice.

About fifteen yards away, she peeked out the side of her house which was practically in her backyard and kind of gave me a head nod as if to say, what the hell do you want?

"Hi, I am selling varsity gold discount cards to raise money for the upcoming football season."

The whole time I am giving her the routine she is shaking her head "no" in disapproval. "All right then, you have a nice day," I said. I smiled and walked away.

Why was this woman afraid of me? Was it a fear of the unknown? Was she a racist? Or was it a combination of the two? I can understand if I knocked on her door at seven o'clock at night and she peered at a dark figure with a smile and two eyeballs staring her dead in the face, but it was two in the afternoon. Yes, I know it's easy to see that black people dominate the prison population, but I have no part in that statistic. I am not a criminal. I've never been in trouble with the law, but obviously she thought otherwise.

On the contrary, I can remember a time a few years before that, when I was about eleven years old. I was young and foolish, but I was aware of the differences between black and white in society. In this incident, I did something to inspire fear in someone. Me, my brother, and two close friends were walking out of a restaurant towards our car. We arrived at the car, and in the vehicle next to us sat an older Caucasian woman in her fifties holding the steering wheel, along with two kids in the backseat. I presume they were her grandchildren. I noticed that she tensed up when we came towards the car and thought it was funny. Why was she so afraid? We are harmless, I thought to myself.

"Yo, this lady is so scared. Watch this," I said to my friends.

I do not know why I did this, but I got really close to the old woman's window, wide-eyed, and glared inside. I could sense the fear when she gripped her hands on the steering wheel even tighter as she tried her best to ignore me. I do not know what came over me, but I barked at her four times as my friends snickered and laughed while entering the car. "I cannot believe you did that," they said as they laughed while entering the car.

I regret it to this day. Maybe this was not her first negative encounter with a person of color, but for her grandchildren, I am pretty sure it was. This episode will probably be etched in their mind for a long time. They might use this situation to evaluate further conclusions they make about black people. I acted like a fool. I wish I had never done that.

When I was in high school, I was really starting to become my own person. The school I went to was in Cranston and it was mostly Caucasian students, but it did have rich diversity. I got along with everyone no matter what race they belonged to. I hung out predominantly with black, Latino, and other minorities. For the most part, I was liked by all, but people told me I was weird all the time.

It was when someone told me I did not "act black," a wrench was thrown into my personality. I was confused. Why do I have to act black? I am black. I thought it was the most stupid thing I'd ever heard, but it affected me. It has since been said every now and again. When someone said it, I would instinctively try to emulate a typical young black male. My personality would shift slightly. I walked with a little more swagger. There goes the salt. My vocabulary would change a little and all my mannerisms were thrown off. I threw a couple of N words into my sentences when I spoke and there you had it. I was now officially black.

I hated that word. I still do. I hated when I did that. I felt like I was not being true to myself. I let society pour their salt on me.

So many people in the real world and in the celebrity world, whether it be sports or Hollywood, have been fooled by the bait and have gotten reeled in to be seasoned with stereotypes that do not embody them. Many images send the wrong messages and people buy into them without deciding in their own mind. They influence the decisions of people in countless aspects of society.

Lebron James is a classic example on the cover of Vogue magazine. They poured salt all over him. Look at him, six foot eight, 250 pounds, holding a beautiful defenseless Giselle Bundchen, body marked with tattoos like the subway in Harlem. The beastly facial expression and the whole frame itself resembles all too well a scene from King Kong. If King Kong were a giant polar bear, would there be a problem? That is beside the point. What I am saying is millions of people see this picture. Now what type of mental decision subconsciously have these people made on how a black man is supposed to look and act?

Many people are salted by their surroundings. They've been hooked by the bait and once they are caught on, it's hard to get off. If you are aware of this occurrence you can escape from it. I have long overcome the previously mentioned comments about me. Whether it be from a white or a black person, when I hear those accusations now, I laugh. It just shows me what those people think of themselves and other people. More than likely, they've taken the bait and have had salt poured all over them. As for me, I will not succumb to such salt statistics. I season myself.

IDENTITY

On July 10, 1998 an eight-hour-old newborn baby girl named Kamiyah Mobley was abducted from a Florida hospital by kidnapper Gloria Williams. Gloria then took her to South Carolina and raised Kamiyah as her own daughter for eighteen years under the new name Alexis Manigo. The biological mother, Shanara Mobley, was grief-stricken, but for eighteen years a small part of her always knew that somehow her daughter was alive. In 2017 through a series of strong leads, police officials were able to DNA test and identify that Alexis Manigo was in fact kidnapped infant Kamiyah Mobley. Kamiyah's kidnapper confessed to her that she stole her from a hospital in Florida and raised her as her own. News stations flocked over this media frenzy as Kamiyah's life went from the ordinary background to the forefront of news outlets. Kamiyah handled every news interview with a smile and grace. She to a certain degree handled it almost too well. No tears or anguish can be overtly detected.

Personally, I thought she was faking it for the cameras, and rightfully so. Kamiyah did not ask for any of the turmoil but she had to deal with it. Behind the smile, poise, and composure was a hurt deep within her. I believe that at the onset of Kamiyah's paradigm shift the seed of an identity crisis was planted. One day she was the daughter of Gloria, and now she had no idea who she was and was conflicted from this since the revelation. The mother who she knew was not hers. Her "father," who believed she was his, was an imposter. Her siblings were not so. Her comforting grandmother was not hers.

The foundation to what Kamiyah thought was her family crumbled and all that was left was an unstable threshold of broken identity, sadness, and rage.

Popular TV network OWN, which was created by Oprah, airs a program called Fix My Life. Fix My Life is a reality television series hosted by life coach and relationship expert Iyanla Vanzant. Iyanla helps people overcome difficult circumstances in their life. Each episode is centered on one problem posed by one guest. Either Kamiyah or someone in her family—kidnapper or biological I do not know—requested they allow Kamiyah to come on the show to deal and heal from her situation.

Iyanla attempted to dig deeper into Kamiyah's feelings but was always met with the same veil of smile and grace. Iyanla knew what was buried inside but Kamiyah continually dodged her psychological advances. Coming close to the end of the day, Iyanla informed Kamiyah's family not to answer her phone calls and told them that if Kamiyah agreed, she would be staying the night at the production house, which was common for certain guests Iyanla felt needed more time. This apparently was the poke that unleashed a tirade.

After Kamiyah learned of Iyanla's method she lashed out not only on Iyanla but also her film crew. She had an arsenal of profanity that the public had never seen in her initial news breaking interviews. She threatened violence, physical harm, but the things she said did the most damage. Iyanla washed her hands of the situation and allowed her to leave and go home. The real Kamiyah revealed herself. She was an angry young woman and rightfully so. I believe her familial revelation was the source of this anger. She had never dealt with it outwardly and when Iyanla pushed, she pushed back. This is the Kamiyah Iyanla wanted to help, but she could not.

When your back is against the wall the true you will be revealed. When backed into a corner, your behavior is a true reflection of who you are. With any internal conflict, if you do not reveal it, you cannot heal it. This is why confidently standing firm in your identity is so crucial. When you know who you are, you cannot be swayed, but life will present you things that attempt to crack at that foundation.

This was the consequence of the lies Kamiyah was told her whole life. I am certain Kamiyah has dreams and aspirations for her life, but I am also certain that an internal chaotic audit of every detail in her life was called into question, leaving her at a mental standstill. She could go through the motions while bearing no self-assurance in her future plans.

I said all that to say this: To fulfill your purpose in this life you must know who you are. When you do not know, or you have a wrong perception of who you are, you do the wrong things and you make mistakes. Having an ill sense of who you are will cause you to make terrible decisions.

In order to know yourself, you must know God. You must know the Father. Your identity is in the Father. If you find your identity in anything else you will fail or all your accomplishments will feel like failure because they do not fulfill you. Too many times we put our identity in things, activities, and job titles, but it will profit nothing.

Validation that comes from stuff is never from God.

People with low self-esteem and low self-worth find themselves trying to prove it to everybody. You wear clothes you think you are supposed to wear. You listen to music you do not even like. You do things you do not enjoy just so you can please people.

For me it was hip-hop, and I am black so I am supposed to dress a certain way. I am supposed to like certain things. I sometimes see pictures of myself when I was a teenager and the clothes I am wearing, and I think to myself, what in the world was I doing. Everything I was doing was to please people. The clothes that I wore were not clothes that I liked but were clothes I thought would help me fit in so people would think I was like them. Even today I deal with this, but I am much better because I am much more comfortable in my own skin. I've accepted me for me. When you are affirmed or feel accepted you are more likely to be comfortable in who you are as a person.

I have some advice for any young men who are in relationships or marriages. If you really want to make your lady feel special, get them a gift. Not for their birthday, not for an anniversary, not for them cooking or cleaning the house, just tell them you got it just because. Women love that, you know why, because it says, your mere existence is what pleases me about you.

Affirmation is so important. People who are affirmed have no problem being themselves. When you know it, you can be, and when you are affirmed in who you are, you can do anything God has purposed you to do.

For this reason, fatherhood is so important for children. A boy who is not affirmed by his father will look elsewhere for it. He'll look for it in other men. They may have lacked affection from their father and so they go looking for that affection in other men, even if it's unhealthy. This can be a reason why young men join gangs or hang out with men who have destructive ways. They long so much for that sense of masculinity they will look for it anywhere, even in unhealthy relationships.

Some young women will get into bed with any man who says they are cute or gives them attention. A girl's relationship with her father is so important for her development and sense of affirmation. A young girl who is affirmed will not be impressed by a boy who says she is cute. "So what if you think I am cute, my dad says I am beautiful." He must put forth more effort to even talk to her.

So what are the keys to knowing yourself? It is far beyond what your favorite color is, or your favorite music album. A massive iceberg floating over a body of water is deceiving because its density is lower than sea water. What you see is not the whole iceberg but only ten percent. The other ninety percent of its mass lies underneath the water. This mass floating through life is you. Your superficial favorite colors or favorite television show is only the beginning. Knowing yourself means respecting your values in life, your beliefs, your personality, your priorities, your moods, your habits, your body, and your relationships. Knowing yourself means understanding your strengths and weaknesses, your passions and desires, your fears and dreams. It means being aware of your eccentricities and quirks, your likes and dislikes, and your tolerances and boundaries. Knowing yourself means knowing your purpose in life.

Do not worry too much. No one is born knowing themselves. This takes self-discovery over time by exploring the inner workings of you. You have to be intentional about it. When you come to those revelations you must confirm it with yourself by verbalizing it. Get familiar with and understand your personality and it will open up so many layers of growth for you. While you have a collective opinion from others around you it's important that you know for yourself what you are like on your own. The true you is who you are when you think no one is watching you. Why do you do the things you do? Why do you react a particular way when conflict arises? Take a peek into your past and how you were raised. You will figure out many of the sources of your actions.

I'll touch upon one example. After reading a book about marital relationships it really forced me to ask some tough questions about my upbringing. I came to the conclusion that I was an avoider. A chronic one at that. I feared conflict and I did not like disagreements. I did not like saying certain things that were on my mind because I had learned not to do it subconsciously. I learned to sugarcoat things so I did not upset people, and people who sugarcoat their hostility cannot grow beyond it.

I began to rummage through old childhood memories to see if I could discover the source. When I was in third grade, I had an itch on my arm. I nonchalantly told my teacher and she told me to go to the nurse. I did not expect that, but also thought nothing of it but to just go. After examining the spot where the itch was the nurse said I had a skin rash called ringworm and it was contagious, so I had to go home. Again, I did not expect that and so my mother had to be called out of work to pick me up. When she arrived she was cold and stoic (typical of my mother).

On our way home from school she went into this rant about how I did not have to call her out of work. I could've waited until I had gotten home from school to tell her about my itch, which I had no idea was ringworm. She would have taken me to the doctor. I was in the third grade. I did not know any better. I then had to listen to her give this same rant to my dad, my siblings, and some of her girlfriends down at the church. I was hurt and ashamed. I had no idea that telling my teacher I had an itch would result in me having to take three days off from school and hearing my mother's complaints told to everyone. It was not only this situation but also others that really put a stamp on my personality.

In your upbringing it's not so much what is taught, but what is caught. After that rant from my mother I had made it up in my mind subconsciously that if I say something is wrong then it will yield negative results, make people uncomfortable, and sabotage people's plans, so I kept things to myself. I learned that if I did not rock the boat everyone would be happy, even at the expense of my own happiness. I learned to be content in situations that I did not like. I learned to say yes when I really wanted to say no. I acquiesced in decisions I felt iffy about. I became a chronic avoider. I was losing myself and also building anger and resentment with people when I just should have spoken up.

I tried to shape shift to meet everyone's demands and it was weighing me down. It reminds me of the story of a chameleon who accidently fell into a box of crayons and exploded. Trying to please everyone will lead to the same end. Those patterns were always safe for me, but I did not see it was hurting my relationships and my marriage more importantly. I thought it was a good thing I was doing all those years growing up, but I realized I had the power to change when I discovered that those patterns were rooted in a negative source of fear and hurt. I became an avoider to appease my mother, my friends, siblings, and everyone I came into contact.

Anything rooted in negative fear will result in destruction. It's very important to detect unhealthy patterns in your personality and that way you can begin a new cycle of healthy interpersonal and inner personal living. More importantly, when you realize where the source of the pattern is you can judge objectively whether it is healthy or not.

One day a father was in the living room watching TV when his four-year-old daughter randomly brought him a teacup full of water to drink. "Here you go daddy," she said, and he thought nothing of it. To appease her he drank it and she walked away. Minutes later she brought him another cup of "tea" and he again drank. He did not give it much thought; he was watching the game and his daughter was behaving.

His brain started to work after the third cup. He realized his daughter was too short to reach the sink. There was no other water source at her level that she had access to, so he followed her quietly and he completely gagged when she walked into the bathroom to scoop out more water from the toilet. He drank with no problem, but when he discovered where the source of the water was, he immediately changed. You have that same power.

Explore where a certain pattern or behavior in your personality is sourced from and the revelation will help you to reverse toxic and destructive ways. In this case, when avoidance becomes a natural part of your interactions with people it will slowly tear apart relationships you hold near and dear to you. There may be times when you may feel that decorating your message in a generous layer of nice will make communication with others better. It may make you feel good temporarily but, when you look closely, communication that is coated with heavy makeup, whether made out of courtesy or flattery, will be counterproductive and endanger meaningful relationships.

DANGERS OF SUGARCOATED COMMUNICATION

You can put frosting on feces, but it is still feces. Sugarcoated communication can take on many different negative traits. It is misleading. It's important to say what you mean and mean what you say. When you say things you do not mean, you are leading the other person in the wrong direction through your interaction.

I was raised by immigrants from Haiti and I had a duplicitous experience when it came to food and culture. Once I stepped into the house I was under Haitian dictatorship and I had to abide the rules and traditions of rulers, my parents. You ate what they put in front of you with no protest. My mother would make this stew called tchaka. The "T" is silent and bears no connection to Black Panther's father. It had beans, corn, pork, and whatever else my mother felt like putting in it that day. I could not stand to eat it simply because it was not very aesthetically pleasing.

I am now an adult and I no longer have to suffer through a bowl of this bean-sauced oppression. Let us say an acquaintance decides to make me a pot of this stew, perhaps as a reward for something I did for them. If I take that pot home and they ask me the next day how it tasted it would not be right if I told them it was delicious, the best I ever had, just because I did not want to hurt their feelings.

If you choose the white lie in that situation, you have definitely saved the sentiments of the acquaintance, but do not be surprised when they make you an even bigger pot of tchaka. God forbid they tell your mother what you said, knowing you fought your mother tooth and nail about eating her stew.

You have to be honest from the beginning. Tell the person, "I really appreciate the gesture and this is not your fault, but I have never liked tchaka. I do, however, love the _____ dish you make. I would much prefer that if you ever do something nice for me."

It is honest and because you communicated it tactfully, the person will respect you even more for telling the truth.

Sugarcoated communication is condescending. If you are convincing yourself that you are being a good person because you adorn your message nicely so that it protects people's feelings, you are not being kind. You are actually asserting superiority over them. It is inconsiderate to think that the person you are engaging does not have the emotional fortitude to handle a message that does not praise them. Another person's emotional wellbeing does not rest on your shoulders. We do not have that kind of power. Believing you do is only a sign that you have fallen into some delusion.

Sugarcoated communication can be passive aggressive. You might choose to say nice things you do not mean because you do not want to be seen as a bad person. You might even use metaphorical ideas to show the real meaning but in a way the person you are speaking with cannot decipher. You might do all this while thinking, "This person just does not get it," or. "Why does not this person understand simple communication?" These are all passive aggressive tactics, and they are meant to protect you from negative effects, and not the other person.

Finally, sugarcoated communication is manipulative, which may be the most dangerous of all. It does not matter what you try to justify your sugarcoating; avoiding the notion of upsetting another person, wanting to sidestep conflict, or desiring to enhance your persuasive power. The end result will be that you change the other person's perception regarding your message in a way that favors you or your own agenda. That is manipulation and at its root it is pride at its best. Be careful not to fall into these methods of communication and it will profit you much in your journey. After all, it is a characteristic of our greatest enemy. Corinthians 11:13-14 says these people are false apostles. They are deceitful workers who disguise themselves as apostles of Christ. But I am not surprised. Even Satan disguises himself as an angel of light. In the way Satan sugarcoats himself to be more palatable for people's consumption, we are not to sugarcoat ourselves or what we say so as to deceive people. It may temporarily appease a situation, but it will ultimately come back up again and even worse. Be true to yourself and other people.

TOXIC POSITIVITY

Looking at the heading of this section you may be thinking, "Is there such a thing?" Yes, there is. Toxic positivity is the excessive and ineffective overgeneralization of happy optimism, and an invalidation of genuine human emotional experience. When a person exudes toxic positivity, they deny any and all negative experiences that make us human and live their life this way. There are certain behaviors that can be signs of toxic positivity either in ourselves or when talking to others. Avoiding and hiding what you really feel can build up a well of negative emotions inside of you. You can pack away so many feelings, but at some point it will have to come out. Kamiya Mobley's story is an example of this.

Dismissing emotions is another behavioral sign of toxic positivity. When you are in a relationship with someone whether it be marriage, friendship, or family, it is important that your emotions are validated or affirmed. It is an important component for healthy communication, intimacy, and love to blossom. This is why toxic positivity is so painful and detrimental to the mind. It involves telling someone that the experience taking place in their mind is not important. This behavior can be so subtle, and many people do not know when it's happening, or worse, think it's normal. When positivity goes too far you can feel like someone is trying to dictate how you feel. Being told you are being too sensitive or dramatic denies you the vast emotional spectrum that makes you human.

Oftentimes the person with TP is not aware or even conscious that they are doing it. If a person is aware that they dismiss others, they do so to manipulate and establish control over another individual. They attempt to make another second guess their thoughts and feelings and push to deny their experience. A more notable term for this is gas lighting. Gas lighting is the manipulation of a person by psychological means, making them question their own sanity.

In this age, "good vibes only" can be so overused, and pitted against someone who genuinely is having a bad day or having a hard time in life. Do not ever let anyone make you feel less for having or exhibiting an authentic emotion. It is okay not to feel okay. It is perfectly fine to be angry. It is not a problem if you do not feel like smiling. Just make sure that those feelings are temporary stops and not destinations.

I grew up in the church world and if someone asked you how you were doing your automatic response was, "I am blessed and highly favored," and, "I am too blessed to be stressed," or at least that is what was expected. God is good absolutely, but you are not required to be jumping with Jesus joy every minute of the day. If that is how you truly feel, by all means, exude that emotion and encourage others, but fakeness and inauthenticity can be spotted by most. Quite frankly if someone is like this all the time, it's clear that they are hiding something.

If you read the Book of Psalms it is of the poetic genre and it expresses a wide range of human emotion simply because it was written by a real person who dealt with real issues. I have so much more appreciation for the Haitian Creole hymns that my parents sang when I was growing up. They meant nothing to me, but now that I am older I have a deeper appreciation for them because of their ability to capture the wide array of emotion that someone can go through in this life. There are songs for sadness, heartbreak, anger, happiness, joy and prosperity. It is okay to not be having a not so great day, and never let anyone rob you of your human experience just so they can feel better. Here are some phrases that may show evidence of TP:

1. It could be worse/I am sure it was not that bad. These statements minimize someone's pain and force TP on them.

2. You shouldn't feel that way. This attempts to assert superiority over someone and denies their feelings or experience by making them feel small.

3. Just get over it/let it go. While forgiveness is a virtue and important for healing and closure, this is an extremely dismissive expression and causes the other person to feel emotionally suppressed and tossed aside.

4. Man up. Men are constantly told this and are indoctrinated into believing that burying one's emotions is manly. This is utterly false and no one, particularly men, should feel that their emotions are strange or unattractive.

Here are some alternatives to toxic positive statements:

Toxic Positivity	Affirmation and Hope
It could be worse / I am sure it was not that bad.	I am so sorry that happened. Is there anything I can do to help?
You shouldn't feel that way	I can definitely understand why you feel that way. I am here to help you through this.
Just let it go / Get over it	Take as much time as you need to get through this and I'll be here when you need me.
Man up.	Man, I've got your back in all of this. You don't have to go through it alone.

While I provided alternate things you can say in tough situations, please understand that saying nothing at all coupled with a warm embrace can do just as much for a person going through a hard time. If you remember the story of Job, after he lost everything he grieved heavily, and I am certain no words could lift his spirits. Job's friends came to see him after all the tragedies had transpired and because his suffering was too great for words, they sat with him on the ground for seven days and seven nights and said nothing. This was a great thing his friends did. When Job was down they got down with him and felt what he felt. This is a true mark of empathy.

Nehemiah is another great example of someone who did not show toxic positivity. Nehemiah, an Israelite, was born in exile in Babylon and when he grew up, he got a great job as a cupbearer under the King of Persia, Artaxerxes. A cupbearer's job was to taste anything before the king did to make sure it was not poisonous. It was a prestigious job and he made great money. One day Nehemiah got word from his brother that his home country Israel was in shambles. The walls of the city were destroyed, and the people were suffering. This caused Nehemiah to be discouraged and the sadness was written all over his face. It affected him so much that King Artaxerxes took notice of this and asked him what was wrong.

Now if Nehemiah was a delusional toxic positivist, he could have sugarcoated it and said he was tired like most of us do, but he was honest about the emotion that he was feeling. King Artaxerxes could have also said, well you are living fine over here in my kingdom you should not feel that way, but he did not. He allowed Nehemiah to leave his job for a long period of time and funded and resourced the rebuilding of the walls of Jerusalem. All this took place because Nehemiah felt and expressed his sadness and King Artaxerxes affirmed what he felt and chose to help him.

Understand that the longer you try to hide your sadness, depression, and low self-esteem, the longer it will take for you to recover from it. In many cases your solution and breakthrough in a matter is on the other side of expressed emotion. Toxic positivity can kill the best of destinies. God cannot, will not, heal the person you pretend to be. At the very foundation of our faith in Christ is the fact that we must admit that we are sinners before a holy God. If we cannot admit that we are depraved, then we cannot admit that we need the savior Jesus and that is exactly why He came. Toxic positivity will get in the way of God trying to do a great thing in you. Your realized destiny is on the other side of your liberated emotion.

UNDERSTAND YOUR CORE VALUES

Andrew Luck of the Indianapolis Colts recently retired from the game of football. During his press conference he confidently admitted that the game was no longer fun because of the cycle of injury that he was enduring. He would get hurt and sometimes have to sit out to recover, but felt the pressure of not playing through it as some expect you to because, "You are being paid millions of dollars to play a game." If he did muster up the fortitude to play while injured, which he did in 2016, he would be stuck in a process of pain and he was not able to enjoy the life he wanted to live. Luck made a vow to himself that he would not put himself through that again. The only way forward for him was to remove himself from the game. Luck had to make a choice between his teammates, coaches, sponsors, and fans, or himself. He made the right decision in choosing himself. The news broke that he would retire during a preseason game where he was on the sidelines. As the news swept through the crowd who attended the game it was apparent that they were upset and disappointed. The most ridiculous part was at the end of the game, as Andrew exited the field, he had numerous cameras crowd around him trying to get the best shot or a sound bite of him answering questions. While this was happening you could hear jeers and boos from the crowd who disagreed with his decision to end his career. The crowd just did not get it. If they had found Andrew Luck alone and unconscious in his home due to a pain med overdose the general consensus would have been, "Why did not he say anything? Why did he not ask for help? Why did he not just retire?" Well that is exactly what he did. Andrew Luck went against the grain and chose himself. When you have established what your core values are and stick to them you will upset the majority and they may shun you but it is better to love yourself and be hated by all than to have the whole world love you and you hate yourself. Why have not you chosen yourself? There comes a point in your life when you have to tell people, "I love you, but I love me more."

Chapter 7
Target Focus

The purpose for a magnifying glass is not just to make things bigger. The unique components of a magnifying glass have been known for many years to create fire. With no matches or a lighter, a magnifying glass is a great tool to ignite a fire. There is a science behind such a natural magic trick. A magnifying glass can kindle a fire from the heat of the sun. This can be done by positioning the glass so that the sun's rays pass through the lens, which forms a small point of light on whatever object you are trying to set ablaze. If the heat from the sun is hot enough, the object is dry enough, and the focal strength of the lens is sufficient, a fire will eventually spark. The science behind igniting a fire with a magnifying glass can be discovered through the study of photons.

Photons are particles that carry and transfer light from the sun to the earth. They also contain energy in the form of heat. Acting as a funnel, the path of these light particles is narrowed to one spot, which is the dot of light that passes through the lens. This results in a collection of heat in one localized area which reaches high temperatures. If a high enough temperature is sustained in that one area, the object that the light is being pointed to will spark and begin to burn. The importance to localizing photons is in the curved shape of the magnifying lens. This shape gathers photons on one side of the lens and funnels them to a single point as they exit the other side. Rightfully so, any item with a convex lens can be used. However, the larger the lens, the easier it will be to start a fire.

The object you want to spark is your goal or objective. The photon energy from the sun is your passion for what you want. The magnifying glass is your focus. Focus is the difference between being mediocre at something and being great in your craft. Focus is what separates you from the rest of the pack. Focus elevates you above the status quo to incredible achievement. At some point in life, if you feel like there is no progress, you must ask where your focus is. If you are not seeing improvement in the things you set out to do, your focus needs to be vetted. Where is your attention being drawn to? To what focal point is all your passion being funneled? Is it producing?

No one says to themselves, I want to destroy my life and be an absolute failure. The detailed decisions you make throughout the course of a day impact the result. Tiny distractions are the culprits for some of the demise you see in the plans you set out to accomplish. One minute you are full steam ahead toward an objective and the next you are sidetracked by things that are not even worth your time or do not contribute to the journey.

One of the difficult things about reestablishing focus is prioritizing what should be done first. Life can be full of menial tasks and keeping them in order can be a challenge even for the most organized person. Life will often bombard your schedule with what feels like hundreds of tasks and planning as to what should be done first can be exhausting and frustrating in and of itself. Every day carries its burden of chores and tasks that consist of answering phone calls/text messages, laundry, preparing meals, feeding the kids, keeping up with deadlines; the list goes on. Too many times our vision can be impaired by having too many targets in front of us and by the end of the day, week, month, or year you realize you have accomplished little to nothing.

I think what many people fail to grasp is the concept of important vs. urgent. It is vital that we zero in on the things that are important and not just the ones that are urgent. Important activities are tasks that have an outcome that leads to us achieving goals that we value, whether they are professional or personal. Urgent tasks demand immediate attention and sometimes involve achieving someone else's goals. They are often the ones we concentrate on and they demand attention because the consequences of not dealing with them are immediate. Knowing the difference between the two can help conquer the tendency to focus on non-important urgent activities so that we can clear enough time to do what is essential for our success.

An urgency led life is stressful and often mimics a person trying to put out hundreds of little fires. By the time it is over you are too exhausted to tackle the important things that matter most. The fact of the matter is we are drawn to the urgent tasks because they tend to be easier and straight to the point, not to mention the reward or payoff of handling it is immediate as opposed to finding out your calling in life, or making a payment to a large debt or achieving great change in a community. It feels good to get things out of the way so you are liberated from the annoying uneasiness of undone tasks even though the endgame, if you continue on this path of urgency, is a life filled up with insignificance.

A study in the Journal of Consumer Research called "Mere Urgency" affirms that when the element of urgency is present, we become less rational in our decision making. The study consisted of a series of experiments where researchers created situations in which they rendered obsolete any reason to choose the urgent above the important—level of difficulty, quickness of reward, and even reward amount. They concluded and found that people still chose the more urgent option. Even when the payoff reward was higher for the important option the urgent task had the higher choice rate. To put it plainly, when a task on your list of to-do's is not easier or not worth as much as a task that takes more time even when there is no reason other than someone has convinced you it's urgent, you will still be biased in the urgent option's favor.

Important vs. Urgent Chart

Quadrant 1 Important and Urgent **Manage**	Quadrant 2 Important but Not Urgent **Focus**
Quadrant 3 Not Important but Urgent **Avoid**	Quadrant 4 Not Important, Not Urgent **Limit**

Quadrant 1 (Q1) Important and Urgent
ACTION PLAN: MANAGE

Quadrant 1 is important and urgent matters, and they are things you must attend to immediately in order to avoid some sort of demise, whether it be financial, personal, or familial.

Examples:
- Transmission fails in your car
- Family member in the emergency room
- Pay speeding ticket before fine doubles
- Meet an assignment deadline at work or school

While things like crises most times cannot be averted, Q1 can be managed with strategic planning. Proactive eliminates procrastination. Do not wait until the last minute to complete a task that should be prioritized early. If you have a ticket fine to pay, the moment you receive it, it becomes an important task but not urgent. When you plan accordingly you can keep these types of tasks out of this quadrant and it will save you the stress of an urgent matter. Your bread and butter is in Quadrant 2.

Quadrant 2 (Q2) Important but Not Urgent
ACTION PLAN: FOCUS

Quadrant 2 is important tasks that are not urgent... yet. This is the ideal place for a task to be categorized. Quadrant 2 tasks are the activities that do not have deadlines that cause extra pressure and life stressors, but regardless help you achieve your important personal, scholastic, and career goals, as well as help you fulfill your overall mission as an agent in God's divine plan. Q2 tasks are typically centered on strengthening relationships, planning for the future, and improving yourself.

Examples:
- Exercise
- Prayer
- Reading to your children
- Writing / devotion
- Practicing a talent/gift
- Studying
- Paying bills
- Taxes
- Date night with your spouse
- School / work assignments

Q2 tasks do not really garner enough attention but this is where your main focus should be. Completing and attending to these activities will make sure that you move through life feeling fulfilled and happy in different aspects of your life. One thing that really gets in the way of conquering Q2 is the fact that you may not know yet what's important to you in this stage of your life. Be careful what and who you devote your time to because you could spend years attending to urgent matters that are not important to you and in the end, you will feel depressed that you have not accomplished anything. You must define what your core values are so that you can pinpoint what path you need to take in life. If prayer is your priority it will not take long for you to realize what it is because God does not do anything without revealing his plan to his servants, the prophets. (Amos 3:7) Q2 is where you should devote the most energy by being proactive and scheduling time for the things you value the most. If you allow Q2 tasks to morph into Q1 emergencies the work you do for Q2 may become low quality. If you are going to grow in destiny you must be intentional. An unintentional life accepts everything and does nothing.

Quadrant 3 (Q3) Not Important but Urgent
ACTION PLAN: AVOID

Q3 are urgent tasks that are not important. They require that we respond to them immediately and they have quick results, but they do not contribute to the overall objective that you have set for yourself. They come in the form of interruptions and are more often than not emergency tasks from other people that help them reach their goal but not yours.

Examples:

- Someone asks you to perform at an event the day before it happens
- A family member who always has drama calls you on the phone to vent frustrations but never has time to listen to your difficulties
- Phone calls, texts, emails
- Getting into a useless argument on social media
- Co-worker wants to spread gossip about your boss during your shift (or ever)

This quadrant can be the culprit of why you feel so busy and tired but unfulfilled. Even if at the moment when you are done helping that person it feels great because they appreciate it, in the long run you feel angry for devoting your energy to everyone but yourself. This is the deception of Q3. It feels important at the moment of request but ultimately, it's only important to the person making the request of your service and over time you can become bitter with people who are further ahead of you because you helped them clear out their Q1 and Q2 tasks, having nothing to show for it yourself. People who have trouble with this tend to be pleasers. They always want people to like them, so they say yes to whatever is asked of them. A sure way to beat this is to become more assertive and begin to use the word No.

Quadrant 4 Not Important Not Urgent
ACTION PLAN: LIMIT AND/OR DELETE
Q4 activities are neither urgent nor important. They are like the top slice of bread that comes in a new loaf, virtually useless. They do not help you increase skill or help you achieve long term goals. Q4's main objective is to distract you and divert your attention away from things you should be doing. If left unchecked Q4 will diminish your destiny.

Examples:
- Surfing the internet
- Watching TV
- Window shopping
- Endless scrolling on social media
- YouTubing religious conspiracy videos

Let us be realistic. I am aware of the world we live in, and social media makes a good pastime. It's great to have when you want to unwind and put your mind on autopilot for a moment to laugh at funny posts and watch the latest viral video, but it must be put on a short leash. I grew up on video games and the way the special effects look; now I know the sophisticated games are very addictive, but there must be a time boundary.

Getting our priorities straight is no easy job and we are often the target demographic for having useless items hurled in our faces, pressuring us to buy, buy, buy. If you have not noticed by now, on your social media feed every fourth post is an ad trying to sell you something. What makes it even worse and a little creepy is those ads are often things you have recently had a conversation about, or Google searched. Your devices listen to the key words you use in everyday interactions, process them, and shoot them right back at you in the form of some pushy ad telling you that you only have a limited time to purchase this powerful showerhead at this low price.

Urgency has been weaponized to get you to make bad impulsive decisions that do not help you on this journey through destiny. Ever since the day I graduated from the University of Rhode Island (URI) I've been getting emails from them urging me to participate in alumni fundraising. Their letters are worded like this: "Time is running out on an important URI Foundation and Alumni Engagement project. I recently sent you several notices because I need your help." Day after day we are bombarded with urgencies that are not important and we must learn to ignore them like I ignore these emails. They are nothing but a waste of your time. It is fake urgency, but marketers do a great job at making you feel that it is worth your attention. They use words like 'ACT NOW' or, 'THIS DEAL ENDS TODAY.'W

It is one thing to know intellectually the tendency to prioritize urgency over importance, but that hardly leads to better choices. The knowing is intellectual but the urgency is emotional or even visceral. As believers, the Holy Spirit can prompt us as to what is of Him and not of Him. The very fact that it tugs at only your emotions should be a sign that it may not be something worth your time. If an urgent matter tugs at your emotions but intellectually you know it is something that will cause you more stress or is not something you value, then you are okay to let it go and drop it. As believers we are warned often in the scripture about how the flesh nature is contrary to what the Spirit wants and the Spirit desires what is contrary to the flesh. Since we know that urgency thrives off pulling on our emotional, visceral strings, we can conclude that unimportant urgent matters are of the flesh nature. If we are not careful, we can easily become slaves to this subtle but overwhelming distraction.

While I am not a fast food junkie, one thing I must admit is that Chick-fil-A has undoubtedly the best waffle fries I have ever tasted and their sauce paired with it is amazing. I've been to all different types of nice eateries that get rave reviews but one thing they have not done is beat Chick-fil-A's deep fried delights. Ironically, while Chick-fil-A remains champion in this aspect, they have never advertised their waffle fries and sauce. As a matter of fact, fries and Chick-fil-A sauce have never really been a focal point of their commercials. Fried chicken has always been the main attraction. Chick-fil-A over the years has done so many different things with how they present their products, but the main thing has always been the chicken.

Make sure that life does not run you off into a tangent. Live in such a way that the main thing remains the main thing. What do you doing most of your days? How do you spend most of your time?

A professor walked into her classroom one morning

and pulled out a large glass gallon jar. Her class watched in curiosity as she then filled the jar with baseball-sized stones until it reached the brim. "Is this jar full?" she asked, and the entire class responded with a resounding yes. She then reached for a bag under her desk and it was full of pebbles that she began to pour into the large gallon jar full of stones. The students watched in silence and some smirked at her next attempt. She filled the jar to the brim with pebbles and then asked again if the jar was full. The student body all agreed now that it was at capacity with another yes. The professor again pulled out another bag, this one full of sand, and began to pour it into the stone and pebble dense jar, while students began to laugh at their naivety. She filled the stone and pebble ridden jar to the brim with sand. The professor asked again, "Is this jar full?" and with more enthusiasm the class was divided as some shouted yes and some no. Finally the professor reached for a bottle of water and emptied its contents into the stone filled, pebble filled, sand filled jar. "Is the jar full?" the professor asked, and the entire room responded with a resounding yes. They understood that the illustration was over but did not know what the meaning of it was. The professor waited for the side discussions to cease and she said, "The point of this demonstration is to show you that if you do not put the big stones in first you will never be able to fit them at all."

The big stones in our life are the things that we value and find important. These things should be your personal relationship with God, family, marriage, and other absolute non-negotiable things that you value heavily. We often in life get this illustration backwards. We wake up in the morning and attack the day by filling the jar of our life with water, sand, and pebbles, neglecting the stones, and when we seek to top the jar with those important stones we find that they do not fit. It is time that we reestablish the proper order of things.

Emails, social media, and accomplishing other people's goals should not be prioritized over the matters that are important and vital to your own life and family. C.S. Lewis put it best when he said, "Put first things first and we get second things thrown in. Put second things first and we lose both first and second things." When things are put in their proper order you can enjoy all of it, but when it is out of place you regret the important things you have missed, and you resent all the urgent things you have answered.

The life of a believer should be an example of this principle lived correctly. Matthew Chapter 6 is the middle of Jesus's famous Sermon on the Mount and here He lectures on prayer and how it should be done. He speaks on the righteousness of men and how we should not do good things just to be seen by other people, but all in humility. He then instructs the people he is addressing not to worry about what they will eat, drink, or what clothes to wear. I find that Jesus attempts to avert our eyes from what is temporally urgent to what is eternally important. He caps off the chapter with something to sum up everything He has instructed and that is to "seek first the kingdom of God and all its righteousness and all these things will be added unto us." These things that we have wrongly prioritized need to be put in the right place and when they are placed correctly, we can then more readily fulfill God's purpose. When we put God first we are saying yes to Him and sometimes that means saying no to other things.

SAY NO

In Book of Two Kings Chapter 3, a new king in Israel, Joram, has taken over and he is not much better than the last king, his father Ahab, who is widely considered to be the worst king of Israel. Ahab, along with his evil wife Jezebel, introduced heavy false god worship into the land and it was outright displeasing to God. Jehoshaphat, our protagonist in this historical account, is king over Judah and is a godly man, but tends to get himself into trouble because he has a problem with compromise.

In this story Ahab has died due to his disobedience and his son, who has taken over, is upset that the king of Moab has stopped paying his regular sheep tax since King Ahab died. Joram is not having it so he takes this urgent matter to King Jehoshaphat of Judah. There should be an obvious response evident to Jehoshaphat—a refusal—especially because he worked with Joram's father Ahab in the past and it landed him in grave danger. God spared him but he did not learn his lesson. Joram asks Jehoshaphat to join him on a siege to take over Moab for their rebellion. Like a broken record Jehoshaphat agrees and says, "I will go, I am as you are, my people are your people, my horses are your horses."

If you are slapping your forehead, you have reacted correctly. Jehoshaphat agrees to attend to an urgent matter that is not important to him and he is willing to put resources, lives, and animals on the line. We too often make this mistake when life throws different tasks at us. Wanting to be liked or accepted by people who do not share the same values as you is a surefire way to land you in major trouble. We exert unnecessary energy on things that are not worth our time. We take on stressful matters that do not even garner a reward in the end. It only leaves us empty, exhausted, and relieved that we lived through it. The first red flag should have been enough for Jehoshaphat to decline. Joram was evil, granted, not like his father, but he was not in God's good graces. We should be careful in partnering with people who are in a wrestling match with God because you and people you love can end up as collateral damage. Some of our greatest mistakes in this life are giving too many chances to people that have proven that their cause is not worth our trouble. There is little to no grace where God has not called you or commissioned you.

Jehoshaphat made the same boneheaded mistake again and made someone else's problem his own problem. So three kings set out to go and fight Moab: Joram, Jehoshaphat, and the king of Edom who is nameless. Given the fact that Jehoshaphat has more battle experience, Joram asks him what route they should take, and Jehoshaphat advises that they travel roundabout through the desert. If you remember from the Long Faith chapter, God took the Israelites the roundabout way to the

Promised Land and that proved to be successful because every step of the way God was with them. He provided food, water, shade from a hot sun and heat for frigid desert nights. It only worked because they were in agreement with and obedient to God. You cannot take the long way without God's approval or favor just because it worked in the past. Understand that when you enter into matters that are not God approved your wisdom, resources, and grace will be in short supply.

Three armies walking and seven days into this desert trip they run out of water for their men and their animals. A seven-day desert trip and they forgot to bring extra water. This is what the evil of unimportant urgent matters will do to you. It will eat away at your common sense. At their wits end, thirsty and exhausted, Jehoshaphat convinces Joram to call Elisha the prophet to get a word from the Lord to answer this situation because—ironically for a desert—they were up the middle of a creek without a paddle. They were too tired to move ahead and too far into this mess to go back and many of us feel like this when we do not stick to our values. That feeling we have in the middle of a mess, "I should've never done this," begins to set in and it feels terrible.

Elisha comes and luckily for them he inquires of the Lord for Jehoshaphat's sake and not for the other two evil knuckleheads. Elisha prophesies that they will not see wind or rain, but God was going to cause water to overtake them and all they have to do is dig holes in the valley they are in. As tired as they were, every man began to dig until they could not dig anymore. After they all fell asleep God caused rushing water to fill every hole that was dug. Every man and animal was replenished and as they filled themselves Moab caught wind of their coming attack and geared up for battle.

As Moab's forces approached the three armies they saw the water on the ground off into the distance but thought it was blood by the way the sun reflected off it, so they assumed the three armies turned against each other. Moab nonchalantly trotted into enemy territory thinking this would be an easy win and the three armies overwhelmed his forces so completely it sent the King of Moab into panic mode. Here is where the story gets weird. Being that Moab is a pagan nation, child sacrifice is a norm and so for whatever reason which I still have not fully grasped, as the war is raging against him and seemingly lost, Mesha, the King of Moab, takes his firstborn son to the top of the city walls and before all three armies he offers him as a burnt sacrifice to the gods. This gesture, as bizarre as it is, actually works. The alliance is horrified by what they see and so they pack everything up and go back home.

They won, but their original objective was to lay siege on this nation for not paying the sheep tax and they left with nothing but bragging rights that they beat the Moabites. After all this calamity and trouble, it left the army alliance with nothing but a long walk home. The victories that you thank God for, was there a reward? What did you leave with when the unimportant urgent matter was attended to? If all you can conclude with is, "Well that was nice," then you have gained nothing and wasted your time.

We often get into situations, trouble comes, and we diligently seek God to answer in the matter. We desire a prophetic word and wisdom from a random person and God will sometimes give that to you to save you, but it does not take all that energy when at the onset of the idea you should have consulted God first or simply should have said no. If it is not something you value, not important to you, or does not aligns with His will for your life, then you do not need God to roll back the clouds to tell you that you should not do something. He has given you enough wisdom through His Spirit to know when to say yes and when to say no. Surely I am not saying you should not help people who are in need, but how are you able to give someone a helping hand if your hands are tied?

Gone are the days when we do for everyone and neglect our own wellbeing. Other people's problems and/or procrastinations are not your problem. If you feel like your life is out of control, running to and fro doing for everybody, neglecting yourself, what you value, and wondering where God is in all this, there is a simple solution that may very well help you: You can find God in your declaration to say no.

Chapter 8
Future Oriented to Present Minded

The Screwtape Letters is a classic novel written by C.S. Lewis which follows a rookie demon named Wormwood. His Uncle Screwtape, who is a veteran demon, sends him frequent letters on how to ruin the life of the human he is assigned to. The Screwtape Letters is a tale of temptation, evil, and sin. Wormwood is in charge of his human's damnation. His Uncle Screwtape sends him tip after tip to accomplish his goal. One piece of advice that Screwtape gives Wormwood regards time and his human's perception and focus on it. Please pay close attention to this excerpt from Lewis's book.

The humans live in time but our Enemy destines them to eternity. He therefore, I believe, wants them to attend chiefly to two things, to eternity itself, and to that point of time which they call the Present. For the Present is the point at which time touches eternity. Of the present moment, and of it only, humans have an experience analogous to the experience which our Enemy has of reality as a whole; in it alone freedom and actuality are offered them. He would therefore have them continually concerned either with eternity (which means being concerned with Him) or with the Present — either meditating on their eternal union with, or separation from, Himself, or else obeying the present voice of conscience, bearing the present cross, receiving the present grace, giving thanks for the present pleasure.

Our business is to get them away from the eternal, and from the Present. With this in view, we sometimes tempt a human (say a widow or a scholar) to live in the Past. But this is of limited value, for they have some real knowledge of the past and it has a determinate nature and, to that extent, resembles eternity. It is far better to make them live in the Future. Biological necessity makes all their passions point in that direction already, so that thought about the Future inflames hope and fear. Also, it is unknown to them, so that in making them think about it we make them think of unrealities. In a word, the Future is, of all things, the thing least like eternity. It is the most completely temporal part of time — for the Past is frozen and no longer flows, and the Present is all lit up with eternal rays. Hence the encouragement we have given to all those schemes of thought such as Creative Evolution, Scientific Humanism, or Communism, which fix men's affections on the Future, on the very core of temporality. Hence nearly all vices are rooted in the future. Gratitude looks to the past and love to the present; fear, avarice, lust, and ambition look ahead. Do not think lust an exception. When the present pleasure arrives, the sin (which alone interests us) is already over. The pleasure is just the part of the process which we regret and would exclude if we could do so without losing the sin; it is the part contributed by the Enemy, and therefore experienced in a Present. The sin, which is our contribution, looked forward.

To be sure, the Enemy wants men to think of the Future too — just so much as is necessary for now planning the acts of justice or charity which will probably be their duty tomorrow. The duty of planning the morrow's word is today's duty; though its material is borrowed from the future, the duty, like all duties, is in the Present. This is now straw splitting. He does not want men to give the Future their hearts, to place their treasure in it. We do. His ideal is a man who, having worked all day for the good of posterity (if that is his vocation), washes his mind of the whole subject, commits the issue to Heaven, and returns at once to the patience or gratitude demanded by the moment that is passing over him. But we want a man hag-ridden by the Future — haunted by visions of an imminent heaven or hell upon earth — ready to break the Enemy's commands in the present if by so doing we make him think he can attain the one or avert the other — dependent for his faith on the success or failure of schemes whose end he will not live to see. We want a whole race perpetually in pursuit of the rainbow's end, never honest, nor kind, nor happy now, but always using as mere fuel wherewith to heap the altar of the future every real gift which is offered them in the Present.

Please note that references to the "Enemy" are directed at God. What really stuck out to me was when C.S. Lewis said, "the future is of all things, the thing least like eternity. It is the most temporal part of time, for the past is frozen and no longer flows, and the present is all lit up with external rays." These are true words to live by. The best place for your mindset to remain is in the present. This can be difficult if you become too goal oriented. Everyone keeps notes whether literal or mental things they wish to accomplish in a certain amount of time.

Often times we can become so obsessed with the destination or the goal itself that we miss the enjoyment of the process or journey to get there. It's important that in the process of chasing goals that we do not miss the details in the middle. Am I saying you should forget your goals? Surely no. I am advising that you do not make your goals a chore. There are things you have accomplished in life that could have been much more enjoyable if you had embraced the "now" of every moment within the process. It is paramount that you focus less on what you hope to do and set your attention on what you are doing.

In the year 2013 I made it a goal for myself to purchase a car. I had my eyes set on a 2008 Dodge Magnum. I was in love with this car. At the time it was a big body vehicle that definitely turned heads. I was so caught up on the end result, picturing myself in the car driving while people watched. I loved the thought of the way I looked in it so much that I hated the current car I had, which was an old busted up grey 1996 Buick Park Avenue. It had no heat or air conditioning. I drove to and from my college campus weekly in cold winters and hot summers with this car. In my mind I was deserving of a "new" car. I was content with the car because it did its job in getting me from point A to point B, but when I made the goal to buy the Dodge Magnum it made me hate my current status. Every time I thought about or saw the Dodge it made me hate my own car. I had to get it. Without changing much in my economic habits, I put enough money away for a down payment to finance it. My focus was so continuously on the end result that when I finally got there, the thrill was gone.

The end result was all I envisioned; never contemplating the financial responsibility it took to sustain it. When the day finally came and I got my car, that is all I was left with. I should have resolved to save money and take advantage of my living situation with my parents. My mindset should have been to build my finances, which focuses more on the journey, the everyday moments toward growth. Had I been more focused on my finances I would have set myself up not just for that car goal but for future goals.

Do not let future goals cloud your mind so much that you miss what is going on right in front you; your daughter taking her first steps, your sister getting her doctorate degree, or your cousin getting a second chance at love. Do not miss these moments, for they are the details along the way that give your goals true meaning. What are your goals if you have no one who is cheering you on? Set your attention on the bright lights of the present and you will always be in a perpetual state of moving forward in joy.

Goals can often create an effect of setting attention on what you do not have. When I was infatuated with getting a new car my focus became about what I did not have. It is great to strive for more, but it made me dissatisfied and ungrateful for what I had. When your mind is locked on the end destination, there is never time to enjoy the journey. When you accomplish a goal, you feel good about yourself, but only until you realize you just lost the thing that gave you direction and purpose. With that you are only left few options: to feel empty and void of any use, enjoy the after-effects of your accomplishments until they bore you, or just set new goals and get caught in the same cycle all over again.

Goals still serve a purpose. Please do not misunderstand what I am saying. I do not want you throwing goals out the window. What I am saying is to create a lifestyle that gets you where you want to go. Focus on the day-to-day. Goals are things you seek to make happen, but the lifestyle and process is the work it takes to get there. It is better to put your energy into building a lifestyle or system. To make a system or lifestyle for a goal you declare what you want to do obviously, but the more important steps are to set up checkpoints that lead you to that destination, create practical steps and integrate those steps into your daily routine.

Let us apply this to something concrete. Let us say you desire to buy a dream home for you and your family with all the bells and whistles. The first thing to do is to transfer that main goal to the back of your mind. Next is to make the necessary steps to changing your lifestyle. Frivolous spending needs to be a thing of the past. Going on random shopping trips has to stop, and do not forget the insatiable craving you have for takeout food. Begin to budget all of your incoming and outgoing money so you can devote your energy to putting money away. Start to evaluate monthly outgoing expenses. Is cable TV really a need? Do you need all those streaming services? Begin to cut out unnecessary spending. This is the new lifestyle and you do not have to obsess over the goal and not having it. Put all your energy into the process and you will achieve far more than just the goal.

It is also helpful to have lifestyle triggers along the way that help you stay the course on this journey. Lifestyle triggers are mechanisms that force you to focus on the process. For example, to keep yourself from eating takeout and blowing your money away, devote energy to cooking at home. When you see food prepared in the fridge that is a trigger for you to keep your money in your wallet and tell yourself that there is food at home. Triggers contribute to the continual focus on the process, which shifts your goal from a far-reaching hope to a present plan of action.

We have for far too long pushed ourselves too hard

for the sake of attaining a certain numerical value on our bank account statement, digital weight scale, certain status in a relationship, degree from an educational institute, or title after your name. The way a goal is set up, most of the time you spend trying to get it, your mind is in a state of failure for all the time you are not achieving whatever the goal is. That will put you in a negative headspace. That state of failure can really turn you away from chasing a goal you set. Oftentimes it will put you in a cycle of disappointment. Let us say you do achieve the goal; the joy of the moment slowly fades as a new goal sets in on your mind's horizon.

I am not sure if this is true for all parents, but growing up the child of immigrants put a lot of pressure me. Like their cohorts they came to the United States for a better life and they sacrificed so much for their children. There is no question they loved their children but many of the aspirations they set for them were overwhelming and caused them to go after things they did not want. Hundreds of thousands of people born from immigrants went after majors they did not love. Nurses, doctors, lawyers, and engineers were the end result, but they were left unfulfilled because those achievements were not their own but their parents'. Even in achieving what their parents wanted for them they were not really able to enjoy the moment of triumph because those moments were often interrupted by the weight of another goal. Parents often are quick to forget about the current victory only to weigh you down for the next task that they want you to accomplish. The day you graduate they will already put the pressure of marriage on you. The day you get married, the weight of giving them grandchildren will be the next load you have to carry, all so you can please them. This is the point where goals can become toxic, hitting target after target only to be left in a perpetual state of unhappiness because you did not make your mark in the time you wanted.

Time can be described in two ways. There is chronos and kairos. Chronos is the natural movement of time. It is the seconds that tick away moment after moment. It cannot be stopped, sped up, or slowed down. We are all at the mercy of chronos. It moves consistently and waits for no one. The second way time is described is kairos. Kairos is different because it refers to an opportune time. It is the appropriate time to do the right thing. For example, lunch is at twelve noon every day at your job. You can only have lunch in that window of time. If you miss lunch that day you cannot get it back until the next kairos moment.

Kairos moments are God moments. God resides in a higher dimensional plain than humans, which means He is not governed by our rules of time. From where He is, God can literally reach from outside our temporal world from eternity and into time at any point and affect change. In this sense, the marking of time is irrelevant to God because He transcends it. This means God does not count time the same way we do. God can see the full scope of a timeline, eternity, past and future. This goes to show that God has total foreknowledge of what your destiny entails. The opportunities and destinations that are laid for you are hinged upon your obedience.

Yielding to the spirit of God will guarantee you see your destiny. When God knows you are ready for something destined for you, He will reach down into your life, take a mundane task like delivering lunch, and insert a kairos moment that will catapult you into your ultimate destiny.

The life of Joseph is such an excellent example of what it means to persevere through adversity and to focus on the present moment even if it is in the midst of difficulty. Joseph had a dream signifying that he was going to be great. Not only did the dream alert him to a promising future, it showed that he would be greater than his entire family. Joseph's obsession with the end result of his dream is sort of what got him into trouble. His father Jacob's deep affection for him did not help the situation either. Joseph was the favorite out of all his brothers because Jacob his father was hopelessly in love with his mother Rachel, but Jacob did not have the same affinity for the mother of his other sons.

In Joseph's obsession with the end result he tells his brothers about the dream he has and how he was going to be greater than them and rule over them. This did not go over well with Joseph's brothers so they plotted against him to get rid of him. This goes to show that you shouldn't be so wrapped up in the outcome of something, because it can lead to unfavorable circumstances. On Joseph's way to check on his brothers as Jacob had sent him to do, the brothers saw him from afar and said, "Here comes the dreamer, let's kill him." After deliberating on his fate they decided to beat him up instead, strip him of his clothes, sell him into slavery, and just tell their father he was attacked by a beast. This set off a set of events that Joseph had no idea he would be facing.

After being sold into slavery Joseph is taken to Egypt and traded to be a servant in the home of Potiphar, an Egyptian officer. God was with Joseph, so he was able to succeed in everything he did even if he was dealing with the anguish of betrayal. Joseph may have been sad about his circumstances but he was not swayed in his mindset. He did not worry about the future or let himself be consumed by anger of the past. He was able to operate in the present moment and do a good job in Potiphar's home. He did such a good job he was promoted to be Potiphar's personal attendant. Joseph gave his absolute best even though he did not like the current situation. Joseph's work ethic pleased Potiphar so much that he put him in charge of his entire household and everything he owned. Because of Joseph's good work God caused Potiphar's house to see even more prosperity. All his household affairs ran smoothly, and his crops and farmland flourished, all because Joseph was not consumed by bitterness and he was used by God to bring favor to his environment.

Perhaps Joseph thought he arrived, and his dream was fulfilled, but that did not sway him from continuing to operate on a level of excellence and integrity. Joseph's mindset remained steadfast. After success it's easy to get comfortable where you are, but you must resolve to stay hungry in whatever pursuit you have chosen.

Joseph was a good looking man and also found favor in the eyes of Potiphar's wife. She lusted after him and when she found an opportunity she attempted to seduce

Joseph into her bed, but Joseph remained loyal to Potiphar and to God about how he lived his life. If Joseph was consumed with anger about his past or too obsessed and anxious about his future, he may have succumbed to the advances of his boss's wife. That is what is often done when we are consumed by anger or anxiety, we seek escape from it. The bed of his boss's wife could have been Joseph's refuge, but he did not fall for it. If there was anyone who could get away with this it was Joseph. He had total control of operations in Potiphar's house. If he wanted to dine at the table of temptation he would only have to declare and command all staff and attendants to some job out in the field away from the home and he could have his fill, but he did not allow lust to cloud his judgment. Joseph sought to honor God with his life. Potiphar's wife made the strongest advances, but Joseph resisted and ran from her as she tore away a part of his clothing.

Hurt by his rejection Potiphar's wife used that ripped piece of clothing as evidence to accuse Joseph of attempted rape. This unfortunate event landed Joseph back to square one—prison. This would make anyone even angrier because Joseph did nothing wrong and it still landed him in an unfavorable circumstance. As a matter of fact, Joseph did the right thing and it still led to his demise, but it was not the end of his story. The Lord was with Joseph even in the prison and it was well with him. This goes to show that even in the most difficult matters God can bring favor over your life if you obey.

Joseph's hard work and excellent management skills impressed the prison warden so much that he put him in charge of all the prisoners and everything that happened in the prison. Joseph must have felt some frustration where he was because he was working in an environment below his standard. Everyone he worked with had a prison mentality while he had previous training under Potiphar's house. God uses situations like this to sharpen your skills and give you necessary experience for the place He has for you. It is difficult to have a palace mentality in a prison environment, but Joseph's work was so efficient that the warden had no more worries because Joseph took care of everything. God caused everything he did to succeed. To the person who feels like their life is a series of five steps forward and ten steps back, if you live a life of obedience God can show you favor even in the most unfair life situations. The key is to remain present-minded in the state that you are in. Work with excellence and integrity and it will ultimately result in triumph.

Not only was Joseph known for his work ethic, but he was famous in prison for his gift at interpreting dreams. He accurately predicted the fate of two men and when one of them, being Pharaoh's cupbearer, was let out of prison, Joseph asked him not to forget him. While Joseph had a present mindset he made sure he took advantage of opportunities in front of him. The cupbearer worked close to Pharaoh and Joseph wanted him to put in a good word. Unfortunately, the cupbearer forgot about him and Joseph had to wait two years until he was discovered.

Now if I was Joseph, I would have been especially upset about being forgotten after I helped someone.

Joseph may have been upset about this, but his anger did not consume him. In moments of difficulty that we do not understand we have to know that our success is not predicated on the elevation of someone else. Do not ever compare your situation to another person's because it will only create bitterness in your heart. Just because God promotes someone in the same position as you does not mean he has to elevate you too. Joseph could have felt entitled because he was obviously more talented and wise than anyone in the prison. God's timing for your promotion does not depend on anything else but his sovereignty.

Pharaoh had a strange dream he could not understand and none of his wise men were able to discern it. This grieved Pharaoh immensely and the cupbearer remembered Joseph and his ability. This was Joseph's moment. They cleaned him up and Joseph presented himself before the Pharaoh and he explained the dream to him. With impeccable tact and accuracy Joseph interpreted the dream in which there would be seven years of abundance and then famine in the land, and Joseph also advised how that should be handled.

Joseph's experience managing Potiphar's house and the prison gave him the experience he needed to answer the matter that Egypt was going to face. Joseph showed divine wisdom in not only handling famine, but more importantly, handling success. Joseph's time in slavery and prison, though unfortunate, was the very experience God used to elevate him to the destiny he saw in his dreams years ago. Pharaoh was blown away by Joseph's wisdom and could sense, even though he was a pagan, that the spirit of God was upon him. In a moment Joseph's circumstances took a full one-eighty turn, all because he remained devoted to excellence and integrity.

NETFLIX AND CHILL

All of the anguish Joseph dealt with wanted to eat away at him and I am certain at some point maybe he thought of his own prison escape. If he succeeded in this he would have missed the kairos moment God prepared for him. If he had checked out of his prison experience, he would have missed his moment of destiny. He would have missed his opportunity to be blessed. There are people currently dealing with unfavorable circumstances and they are literally fighting God and do not even know it. You may think because the experience that you are in is unpleasant, you want it to end or somehow change, but God uses unpleasant, unfavorable "prison" experiences to shape you so that you will be ready for the kairos. I want to assure you that you have not missed a thing. You are right on schedule for a kairos moment. A lot of chronos time may have passed, but through your obedience, God is orchestrating your kairos moment.

I have this wonderful device at home called an Amazon fire stick. Like most people I have a Netflix subscription and I can watch a plethora of TV shows. My wife and I got married in July of 2015. My wife and I had a favorite TV show we watched only available through Netflix, which is The Office. There were nine seasons of this show that aired from 2005-2013. We never knew about this show when it aired in the kairos time that it was on TV. We missed it but because of Netflix we were able to watch the whole of the sitcom that took eight years to make in its entirety in the span of a few months. God is in the business of redeeming the chronos you felt has been wasted by betrayal and bad circumstances you have been dealt.

When Joseph stood before the powerful world leader Pharaoh, he had no idea his life was about to change. After interpreting Pharaoh's dream and giving him wise counsel, Pharaoh knew that Joseph was the man for the job. He made Joseph second in command over all of Egypt. He put his signet ring on Joseph's finger. He dressed him in royal clothing and put a gold chain around his neck. He then gave Joseph second chariot to provide transportation. He gave him a new name and a beautiful wife all in a moment. Know that when you walk in obedience God is in the business of redeeming the time you feel you have lost to betrayal, mistakes, and challenging circumstances. In a moment's notice God can remove you from that place in which you feel stuck. When you obey, God has the ability to Netflix your time. He can take you from a prison to a palace, put a ring on your finger, help you find a spouse, give you a new mode of transportation, and give you a new job position even though you never applied. What you think will take years to complete you can accomplish in less time if you submit to obedience to God. Your triumph may not happen exactly like Joseph's story, but model the excellence that he lived by because it will profit you much. God can Netflix your destiny; just chill, take heart, and trust the process.

Chapter 9
Don't Miss The Shift

I hope that I have done my due diligence in helping you see that at any moment God can literally change you or any life circumstance. Obedience to Him is your most powerful weapon in this journey through destiny. Sometimes obeying God will call for you to leave some things behind, abandon people, and shed certain devices and methods that will not help you in the next phase of life. With these principles you should be able to see clues that help you identify where transition is. No longer will specific events be just happenstance, but instead will be catalysts to new levels in your life.

In times of transition, do not let your environment or people around you discourage you from moving forward. People's concerns about your wellbeing can be a point they use to hold you back. They will say things like, it is too risky or too dangerous, but if you are steadfast in what you know God has called you to do you will not be put to shame. Shortcomings and disabilities will always be apparent, but that is exactly what makes God so great. He uses us and our imperfections to exhibit how powerful He can be in someone's life who obeys and diligently seeks Him. Do not wait to do what you know He told you to do because delayed obedience is disobedience.

Also, understand and know that great things take time and shortcuts only diminish the quality of a finished product. There is no rushing when it comes to the will of God. Everything moves at a pace that is set by His grace. Every step of the way make sure you consult God about what is happening next and He'll never steer you in the wrong direction. Things may look terrible, but better you rejoice through hell with God having just enough, rather than being in abundance and not having the presence of God to accompany you on this journey.

The most troubled times of David's life were when he was the closest to God. He consulted him on everything he was doing. Some of his greatest psalms were written when he was being hunted and tracked down by a psychotic king. David took refuge in God. His greatest mistakes happened when he was in abundance and got comfortable in the state that he was in.

Troubles and suffering keep us humble. Do not always preoccupy your prayers with declarations to God to get you out of a certain matter. Pray for His wisdom to endure through the hard days and He will show Himself strong and mighty on your behalf for His glory. Do not let the opinions and perspectives of people ruin your vision on what God is doing with you. This calls for you to remain true to yourself and your values.

The more you draw closer to God, the more near He will draw to you, and you never encounter God without Him telling you who you are. He always reminds those He called that they were men and woman of valor. He called them to be leaders in situations that were calamitous. God called people to speak when they felt their words were not eloquent. God called people to fight large armies even though they felt they were too small. He always called and told them who they were. On this journey through destiny God will show you exactly who you are. Always be real with God because He will not use the person you pretend to be.

In this time your vision will be focused and you will have a better understanding on what God wants you to do. No longer will you be at the mercy of daunting tasks that have nothing to do with your values or God's will. Your target will be His glory alone. Because your target is focused your present walk with Him will be clearer. Overwhelming burdens of future goals will not drag you in circles anymore. When worries of the future may have caused impulsive behavior you can now empty those burdens at God's throne. Your present walk with Him should always be where your focus remains. If His word is a lamp to your feet and a light to your path then you do not have to worry about what is far ahead, only what is directly in front of you. This will be the reassurance you will need when you face hardship.

Much of it will be unfair and you will feel like God is against you but if you hold fast to what He told you and showed you, surely He who began a good work in you will bring it into completion. You just have to trust what He is doing.

In times of trouble you can find some parallel within the story of the Israelites' time in the wilderness and your own life. I covered their initial escape from Egypt and some instances of their wilderness journey, but we all know from the story that they spent forty years there. I find that to be very interesting because all throughout scriptures God's will often involves the number forty. I believe it to be intentional. It rained for forty days and forty nights in the story of Noah. Moses spent forty years in the desert before God called him to free his people. He also spent forty days and nights on Mount Sinai alone communing with God. Elijah walked forty days in the desert and encountered God. Ezekiel laid on his right side for forty days to bear the iniquity of Israel and Judea. Goliath taunted Israel for forty days before David defeated him and set a trajectory for his journey to the throne. Jesus fasted for forty days in the desert while being tempted by Satan and when He passed through it, He began His miraculous ministry. Jesus also spent forty days on earth after His resurrection and was seen by men before He ascended to the right hand of God.

All of these examples show me that God uses the number forty to signify a time of judgment, a time of test and trial, a change in generation, but most of all it represented transition. Forty mars some sort of isolation, change, and lets you know that there is a shift in progress. It is a time of great change.

Why am I saying all of this? I wrote much of this book while in quarantine from a global pandemic. If you look up the word "quarantine" it has origins in Latin and French. It means forty. It even sounds like forty in the actual word if you are bilingual. Am I saying that every time you see the number forty in your everyday life it signifies some divine appointment? Surely no. The quarantine did not last forty days, but I felt it led to this point when I was preparing this book for you. When the Israelites came out of Egypt, God used a series of plagues and epidemics to get their attention. I do not necessarily think God caused this epidemic, but I strongly believe that God was using this period as a time of judgment, a time of test and trial and a change in the way we do things, not only for the world but for His church and ultimately you.

I do not believe things will be the same in our churches or your personal life. I believe God is going to do unconventional things with his people. God is going to upset a lot of people who are used to tradition and the way things are usually done. You think God will go left but he will go right. Do not miss the shift that is in progress. Do not miss the transition God is going to bring in your own life.

When your time of isolation is finished things will not be the same. When God's appointed time for your isolation has ended, you will not be the same. You need long faith in this time. You need to know that God always keeps his promises as long as you obey Him. You need to follow the fire of his presence. You have to stick close to him if you want to see the benefits of it. Never waste a grand transition or you can be left behind in what God is going to do. Above all else fear can be a great hindrance in all of this, and it is the final obstacle I present to you that fear needs to be conquered.

In my early to mid-twenties my wife and I were just dating, and we were a part of the same worship band. We normally practiced on Saturdays and on this day we were expecting a snowstorm to arrive. The inclement weather started about thirty minutes to an hour before we left so there was significant snow on the ground as we cancelled the rest of practice. I was driving an old busted up Buick and my wife then girlfriend was driving a Jeep Liberty SUV. She lived an hour out of state so we resolved that she would follow me home until the roads were plowed enough for her to make it safely to Boston. We started on our route and after being on the highway for a mile or so I noticed that she was not behind me anymore. I started to wonder where she could have gone, but perhaps she took a different way to my parents' house. Soon after I received a call on my cellphone, and it was my wife Charlene. I asked her where she was and what happened. With what sounded like tears in her eyes she asked me why I left her.

Me being the impatient person that I am (God's still working on me) I denied leaving her and said we had to be home before we got stuck out there. I asked her where she was, and she said she took the nearest exit because she was scared. While driving, her car began to lose traction on the road and she was fishtailing. She felt like she could not keep up, so she pulled into the nearest parking lot and stayed there. I've since apologized for it, but I was annoyed because I just wanted to be home. I needed long faith that night. I drove to where she was in that bank parking lot and as I approached, I was already covered in snow.

I reached and pulled the door open and there she was with the car running, tears in her eyes. I had totally forgotten that less than a year prior to that date she was in a terrible highway accident. Her brakes failed and her car flipped on the highway. I was on the phone with her while it happened as it was our custom to stay on the phone when either of us drove the hour ride home. It was inconsiderate of me to not be mindful of the fact that she was recently in a terrible accident. As she was driving in the snow and felt the loss of control she got off the road she was on and was at a standstill.

With the car door open and snow accumulating on the ground I looked at her and said one thing: "You have four-wheel drive." I then reached across her lap, and right next to her gearshift was another lever, which was the shift that put her into the superior four-wheel drive. I told her that it gave her the ability to gain control of her car where other vehicles might lose traction. I then made her do a few laps in the lot to show her the difference and we made it home safely.

I say all this because this very instance may have happened or is happening to you right now. You were on a road and because of the fear of a past experience you took the nearest exit off that road of destiny to park and just sit there, overtaken by fear. This is a final reminder to you that there is a shift in you, and you are equipped with something more powerful than any vehicle. It is God's Holy Spirit guiding you through this life and if you would only put your trust in Him, he will see you through the worst of circumstances. Unlike the vehicle, the Holy Spirit is not some powerful force; He is a mighty and valiant companion to you, ready to assist you in the most difficult of life situations. When you are confused, He can bring clarity. When you are afraid, He will give you courage. Best of all when you are at your wit's end and do not know what to pray for, He will pray for you, discerning the Father's will for your life. At this point in your life, it is time to pull the proverbial lever on your destiny and put His word into practice. Ready. Set. SHIFT.

www.ingramcontent.com/pod-product-compliance
Lightning Source LLC
Chambersburg PA
CBHW071215160426
43196CB00012B/2319